Fill the House with Cross-Stitch

Fill the House with Cross-Stitch

Catherine Austin

A Sterling/Chapelle Book
Sterling Publishing Co., Inc. New York

Owner
Jo Packham

Staff
Trice Boerens, Gaylene Byers,
Holly Fuller, Cherie Hanson, Susan Jorgensen,
Margaret Shields Marti, Jackie McCowen,
Barbara Millburn, Pamela Randall,
Florence Stacey, Nancy Whitley
and Lorrie Young

Photographer
Ryne Hazen

The photographs in this book were taken at Mary Gaskill's
Trends and Traditions and at the home of Jo Packham. Their friendly
cooperation and trust is deeply appreciated.

Library of Congress Cataloging-in-Publication Data

Austin, Catherine.
    Fill the house with cross-stitch / by Catherine Austin.
       p. cm.
    "A Sterling/Chapelle book."
    Includes index.
    ISBN 0-8069-0620-0
    1. Cross-stitch—Patterns. I. Title.
TT778.C76A9 1994   93-39095
746.44'3—dc20   CIP

10 9 8 7 6 5 4 3 2 1

A Sterling/Chapelle Book

Published by Sterling Publishing Company, Inc.
387 Park Avenue South, New York, N.Y. 10016
© 1994 by Chapelle Ltd.
Distributed in Canada by Sterling Publishing
℅ Canadian Manda Group, P.O. Box 920, Station U
Toronto, Ontario, Canada M8Z 5P9
Distributed in Great Britain and Europe by Cassell PLC
Villiers House, 41/47 Strand, London WC2N 5JE, England
Distributed in Australia by Capricorn Link (Australia) Pty Ltd.
P.O. Box 6651, Baulkham Hills, Business Centre, NSW 2153, Australia
Printed in Hong Kong
All rights reserved

Sterling ISBN 0-8069-0620-0

Welcome to a house full of cross-stitch!

The combination of embroidery floss and fabric in cross-stitch
—a simple stitch—become the tools for creating artistic color and design. With
these tools, you, the artist, can create the delightful projects that fill the pages of
this book, projects that are sure to add a special feeling of warmth and
hand-crafted beauty when placed in the rooms of your home.

For the nursery, a cozy airplane blanket will keep your little one
bundled in clouds all night long. A cross-stitched picture mat of mallard
ducks among cattails is the perfect complement to the rustic atmosphere of the
den. Decorate for Christmas with stockings on the mantle. In the kitchen,
sachet bags filled with potpourri will smell as pleasant as they look
when cross-stitched with delectable designs of fruit.

All of these treasures and much, much more are in store for you and your
cross-stitching pleasure to fill every room in your home.

CHAPTER ONE

LIVING ROOMS

NORTH WOODS STOCKING

Supplies

Completed cross-stitch on Fiddlers Cloth 14
⅜ yard of green fabric; matching thread
½ yard of fleece
1 yard of narrow cording

Directions

All seams are ¼".

1. Enlarge stocking on grid to make full-size pattern. From stitched design piece, cut one stocking front with top edge of design ¾" below and parallel to top edge of pattern. From green fabric, cut one stocking front, two stocking backs and one 2" x 5" piece for hanger. Also from green fabric, cut 1¾"-wide bias strips, piecing as needed to equal 1 yard. From fleece, cut two stockings.

2. Make 1 yard of corded piping. With raw edges aligned, stitch the piping down the side, around the bottom, and up the other side of the stocking front. Baste one fleece stocking to wrong side of stocking front. Repeat for back. With right sides facing, stitch the stocking front to the back, sewing along the stitching line of the piping. Leave top edge open.

3. To make lining, stitch remaining green stocking front and back together, with right sides facing and leaving top edge open and a small opening in side seam above heel.

4. To make hanger, fold hanger piece in half with long edges matching. Stitch long edges. Turn. Fold to make 2½" loop. With raw edges matching, pin the hanger to the top right side seam of the stocking.

5. Slide lining over stocking, matching top edges and side seams. Stitch top edge, securing hanger. Turn through opening in lining. Slipstitch opening closed. Stuff lining inside stocking.

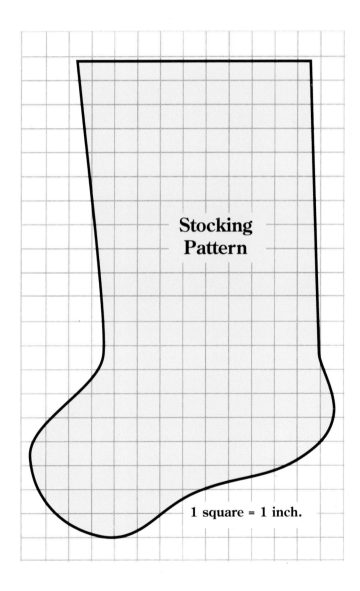

Stocking Pattern

1 square = 1 inch.

Stitch Count: 121 x 194

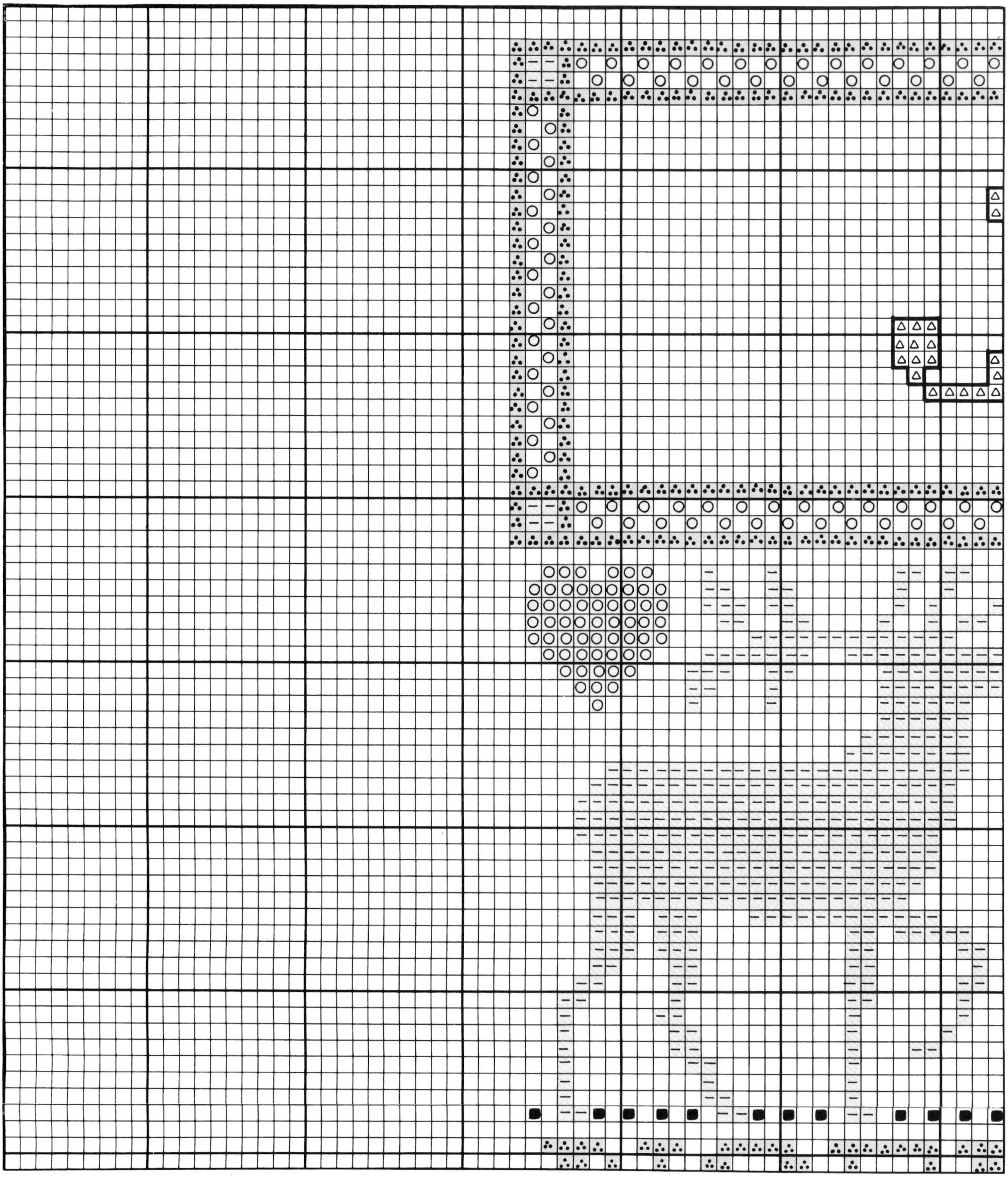

13

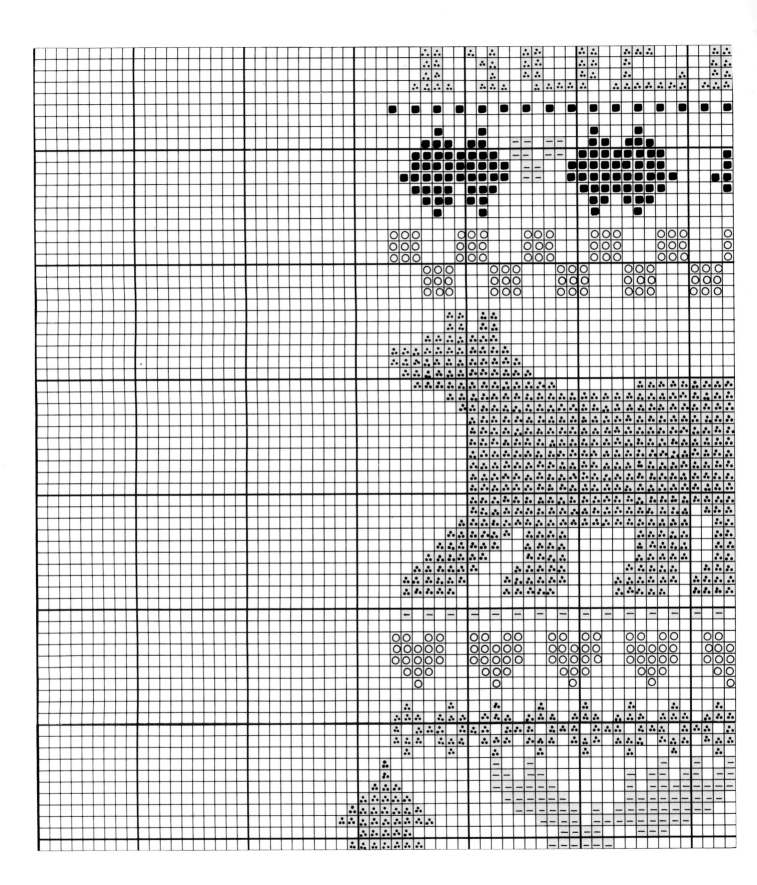

14

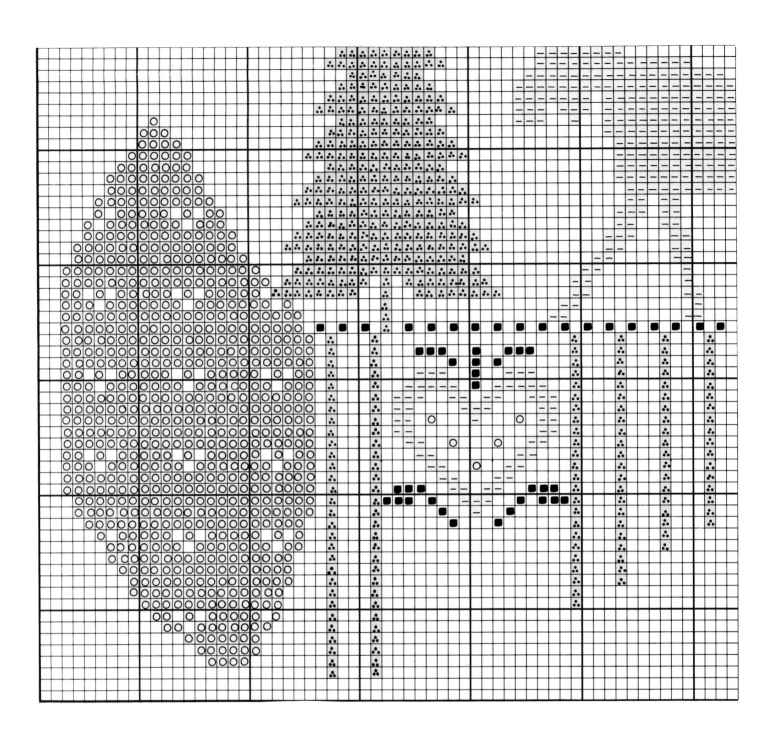

16

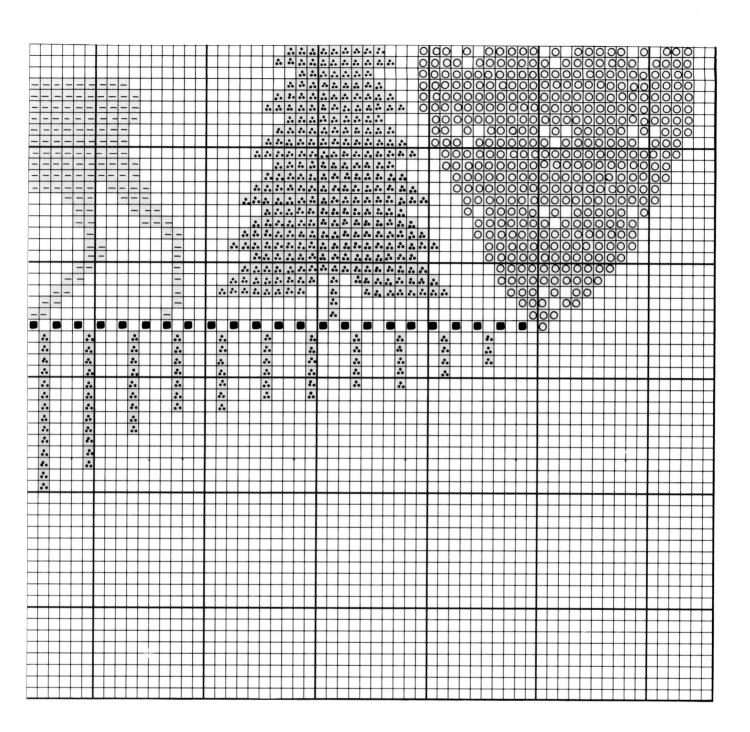

LIVING ROOMS

Stitched on Fiddlers Cloth 14 over one thread, the finished design size is 8⅝" x 13⅞". The fabric was cut 13" x 18".

FABRIC	DESIGN SIZE
Aida 11	11" x 17⅝"
Aida 14	8⅝" x 13⅞"
Aida 18	6¾" x 10¾"
Hardanger 22	5½" x 8⅞"

Anchor   **DMC (used for sample)**

Step 1: Cross-stitch (2 strands)

Anchor		DMC	
47	⊙	321	Christmas Red
210	■	562	Jade-med.
879	∴	500	Blue Green-vy. dk.
879	△	500	Blue Green-vy. dk. (alphabet)
380	−	839	Beige Brown-dk.

Step 2: Backstitch (1 strand)

47		321	Christmas Red

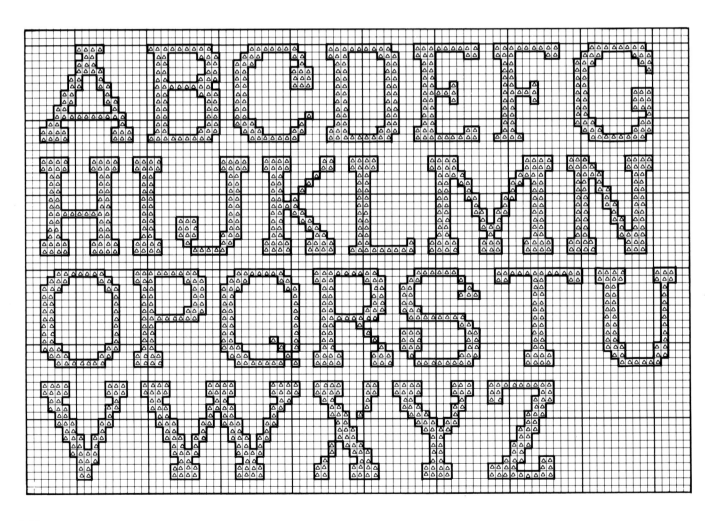

NORTH WOODS SAMPLER

LIVING ROOMS

Stitched on Ragusa 14 over one thread, the finished design size is 8¾" x 14⅛". The fabric was cut 15" x 21".

FABRIC	DESIGN SIZE
Aida 11	11⅛" x 18"
Aida 14	8¾" x 14⅛"
Aida 18	6⅞" x 11"
Hardanger 22	5⅝" x 9"

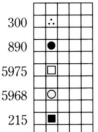

Anchor		DMC (used for sample)	
Step 1: Cross-stitch (2 strands)			
300	∴	745	Yellow-lt. pale
890	●	729	Old Gold-med.
5975	□	356	Terra Cotta-med.
5968	○	355	Terra Cotta-dk.
215	■	320	Pistachio Green-med.

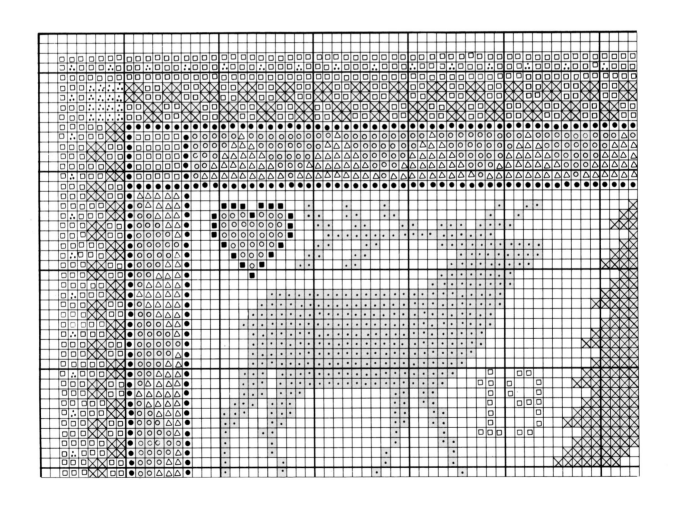

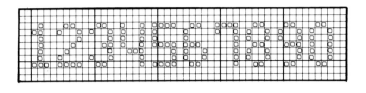

875	△		503	Blue Green-med.
878	✕		501	Blue Green-dk.
381	•		838	Beige Brown-vy. dk.

Stitch Count: 123 x 198

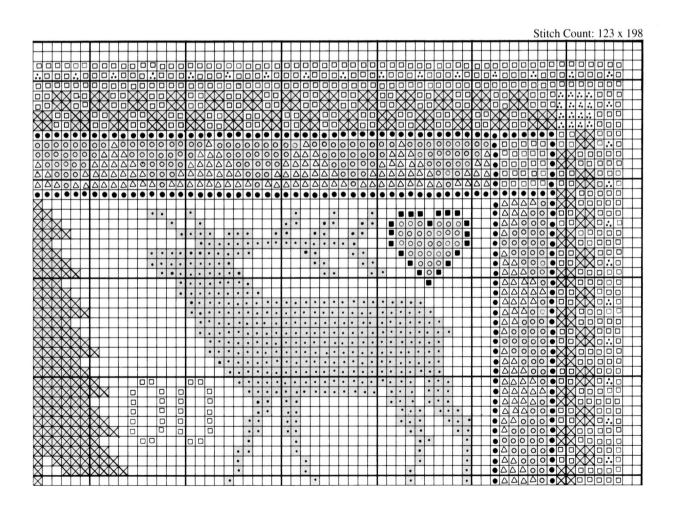

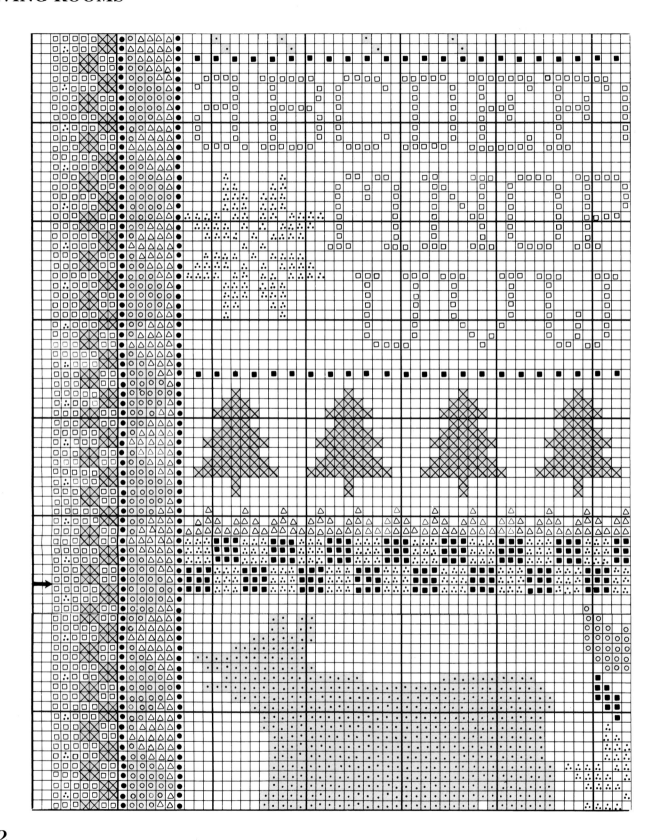

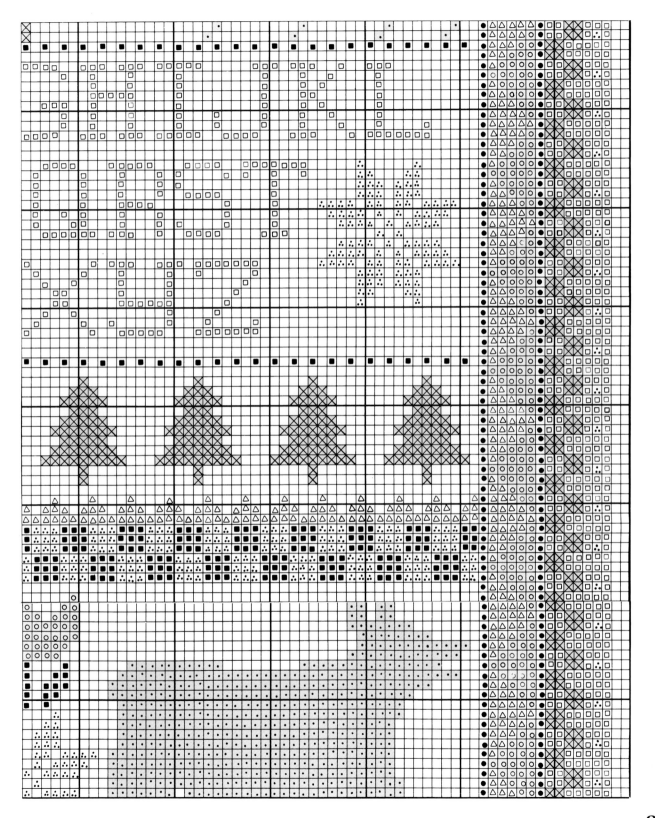

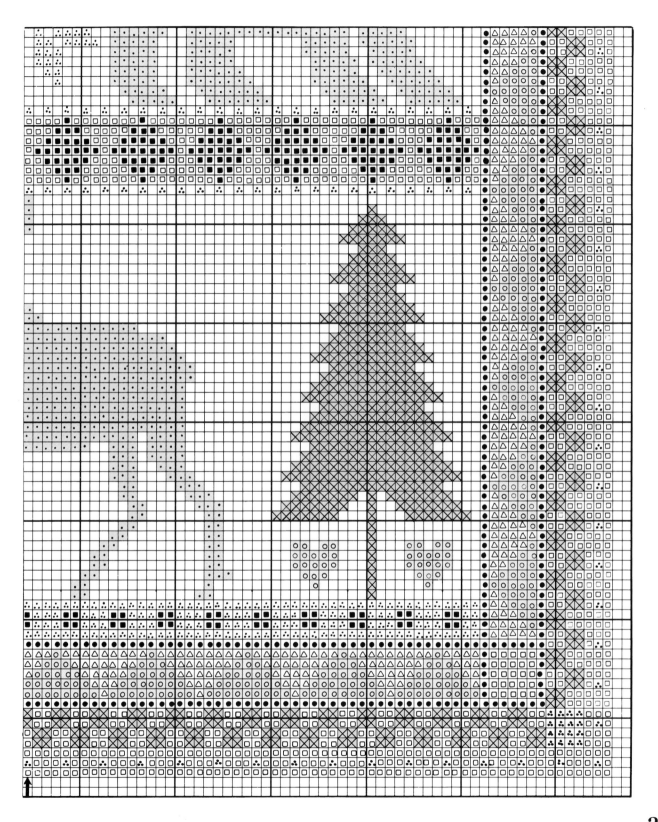

BORDER SAMPLER PILLOW

Supplies

Completed cross-stitch on Celadon Aida 18
³⁄₈ yard of dark green fabric; matching thread
¹⁄₈ yard of light green fabric; matching thread
1½ yards of narrow cording
One 14" x 14" pillow form

Directions

All seams are ¼".

1. With design centered, trim design piece to 7" x 7½". From dark green fabric, cut one 13" x 13½" piece for back and four 3½" x 10¾" pieces for front border. From light green fabric, cut 1½"-wide bias strips, piecing as needed to equal 1½ yards.

2. Make piping; set aside. With right sides facing, and one side and one long edge aligned, stitch one border piece to one edge of design piece, stopping 1" from corner of design piece. Repeat with remaining border pieces, stitching each to one entire edge of design piece; see Diagram. Return to first border piece and complete seam.

```
┌─────────────┐
│  ┌───────┐  │
│  │       │  │
│  │Stitched│ │
│  │ Piece  │ │
│  │       │  │
│  └───────┘  │
│             │
└─────────────┘
```

Diagram

3. With right sides facing and raw edges aligned, stitch piping around all edges of pillow front. Clip seam allowance of piping at corners. With right sides facing, stitch pillow front to pillow back, sewing along stitching line of piping and leaving one edge open. Trim corners and turn. Insert pillow form and slipstitch opening closed.

Stitched on Celadon Aida 18 over one thread, the finished design size is 5½" x 6". The fabric was cut 11" x 11".

FABRIC	DESIGN SIZE
Aida 11	9" x 9⅞"
Aida 14	7⅛" x 7¾"
Hardanger 22	4½" x 5"

Anchor		DMC (used for sample)	
	Step 1: Cross-stitch (1 strand)		
49	ı	963	Wild Rose-vy. lt.
66	✕	3688	Mauve-med.
42	●	3350	Dusty Rose-dk.
101	∴	327	Antique Violet-vy. dk.
145	·	334	Baby Blue-med.
878	□	501	Blue Green-dk.
246	○	895	Christmas Green-dk.

Stitch Count: 99 x 109

HEAVENLY TIMEKEEPER

LIVING ROOMS

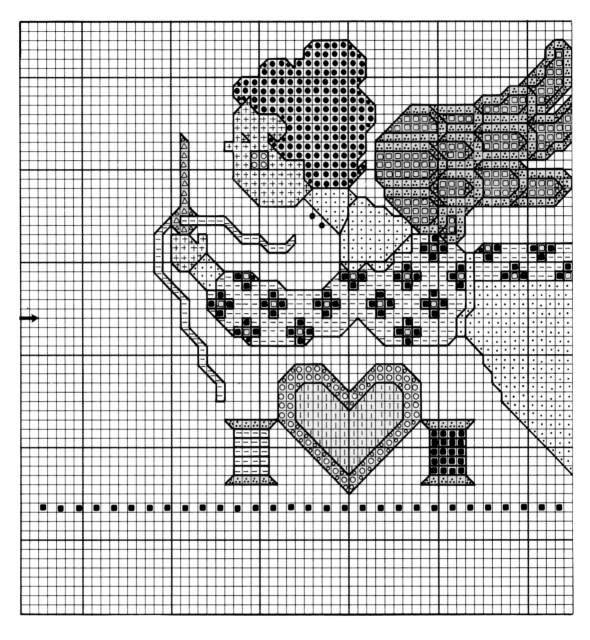

Stitched on Aqua Yorkshire 14 over one thread, the finished design size is 8⅝" x 4¼". The fabric was cut 13" x 10". Insert design piece in clock, following manufacturer's instructions.

FABRIC	DESIGN SIZE
Aida 11	11" x 5½"
Aida 14	8⅝" x 4¼"
Aida 18	6¾" x 3⅜"
Hardanger 22	5½" x 2¾"

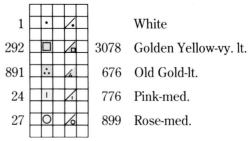

Anchor		DMC (used for sample)

Step 1: Cross-stitch (2 strands)

Anchor		DMC	
1			White
292		3078	Golden Yellow-vy. lt.
891		676	Old Gold-lt.
24		776	Pink-med.
27		899	Rose-med.

30

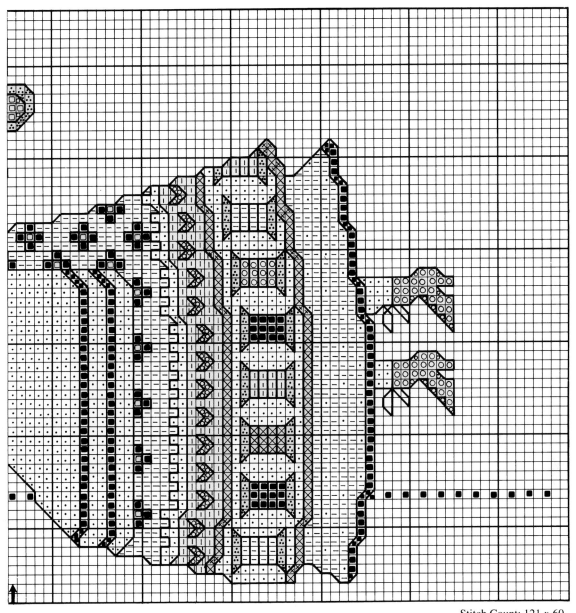

Stitch Count: 121 x 60

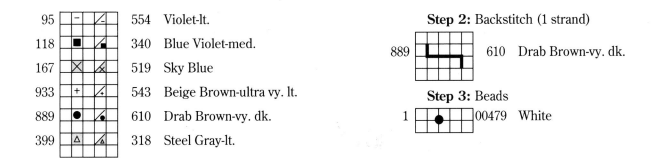

95	554	Violet-lt.
118	340	Blue Violet-med.
167	519	Sky Blue
933	543	Beige Brown-ultra vy. lt.
889	610	Drab Brown-vy. dk.
399	318	Steel Gray-lt.

Step 2: Backstitch (1 strand)

| 889 | 610 | Drab Brown-vy. dk. |

Step 3: Beads

| 1 | 00479 | White |

VARIEGATED PILLOW

Supplies

Completed design on Cream Klostern 7;
   matching thread
⅜ yard of unstitched Cream Klostern 7
Liquid ravel preventer
⅜ yard of print fabric; matching thread
2½ yard of small cording
Dressmaker's pen
12" x 12" box pillow form

Directions

All seams are ¼".

1. With design centered, trim design piece to 10¼" x 10¼" for pillow front. Treat edges with ravel preventer. From unstitched Klostern 7, cut one 3¼" x 37½" strip for pillow gusset and one 10¼" x 10¼" piece for pillow back. Treat edges with ravel preventer. From print fabric, cut 1½"-wide bias strips, piecing as needed to equal 2½ yards. Make piping.

2. With right sides facing and raw edges aligned, stitch piping to pillow front and back, rounding corners slightly.

3. With right sides facing and raw edges aligned, stitch one long edge of gusset to pillow front along stitching line of piping, rounding corners. With right sides facing, stitch short edges of gusset together.

4. Stitch pillow back to gusset along stitching line of piping, leaving a 3" opening above one corner. Clip curves and turn through opening. Insert pillow form and slipstitch opening closed.

Stitched on Cream Klostern 7 over one thread, the finished design size is 6¾" x 6¾". The fabric was cut 14" x 14".

FABRIC	DESIGN SIZE
Aida 11	4¼" x 4¼"
Aida 14	3⅜" x 3⅜"
Aida 18	2⅝" x 2⅝"
Hardanger 22	2⅛" x 2⅛"

Watercolours (used for sample)

Step 1: Cross-stitch (1 strand)

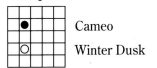

Cameo

Winter Dusk

LIVING ROOMS

Stitch Count: 47 x 47

SHIP SAMPLER

LIVING ROOMS

Stitched on Champagne Linen 28 over two threads, the finished design is 9" x 8". The fabric was cut 15" x 14".

FABRIC	DESIGN SIZE
Aida 11	11½" x 10⅛"
Aida 14	9" x 8"
Aida 18	7" x 6¼"
Hardanger 22	5¾" x 5⅛"

Anchor   **DMC Flower Thread (used for sample)**

Step 1: Cross-stitch (1 strand)

I	Ecru
+	2743 Yellow-lt.

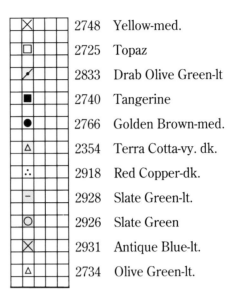

	2748	Yellow-med.
□	2725	Topaz
╱	2833	Drab Olive Green-lt.
■	2740	Tangerine
●	2766	Golden Brown-med.
△	2354	Terra Cotta-vy. dk.
∴	2918	Red Copper-dk.
–	2928	Slate Green-lt.
○	2926	Slate Green
⊠	2931	Antique Blue-lt.
△	2734	Olive Green-lt.

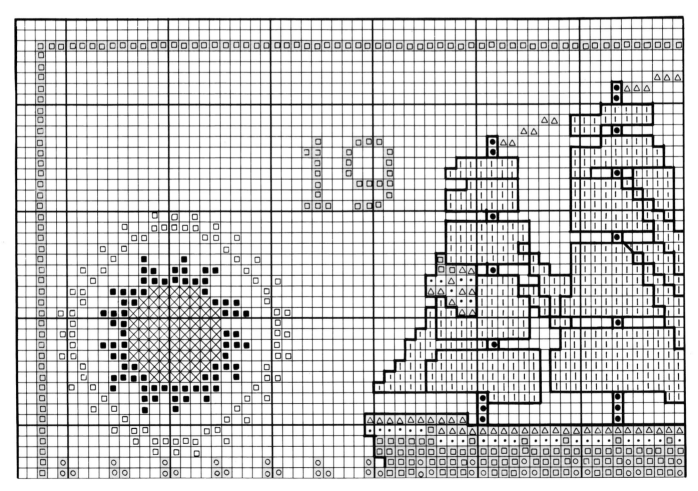

36

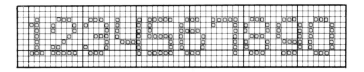

2732   Olive Green

2938   Coffee Brown-ultra dk.

2280   Shell Gray-lt.

DMC Floss
Step 2: Backstitch (1 strand)

3371   Black Brown

DMC Floss
Step 3: French Knot (1 strand)

3371   Black Brown

Stitch Count: 126 x 112

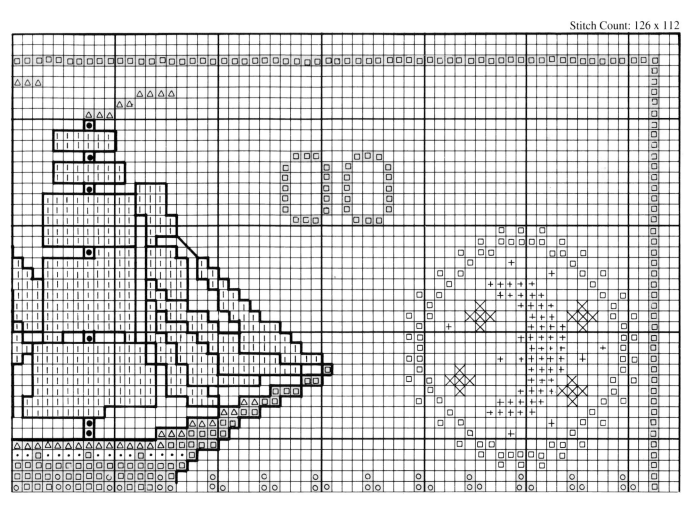

37

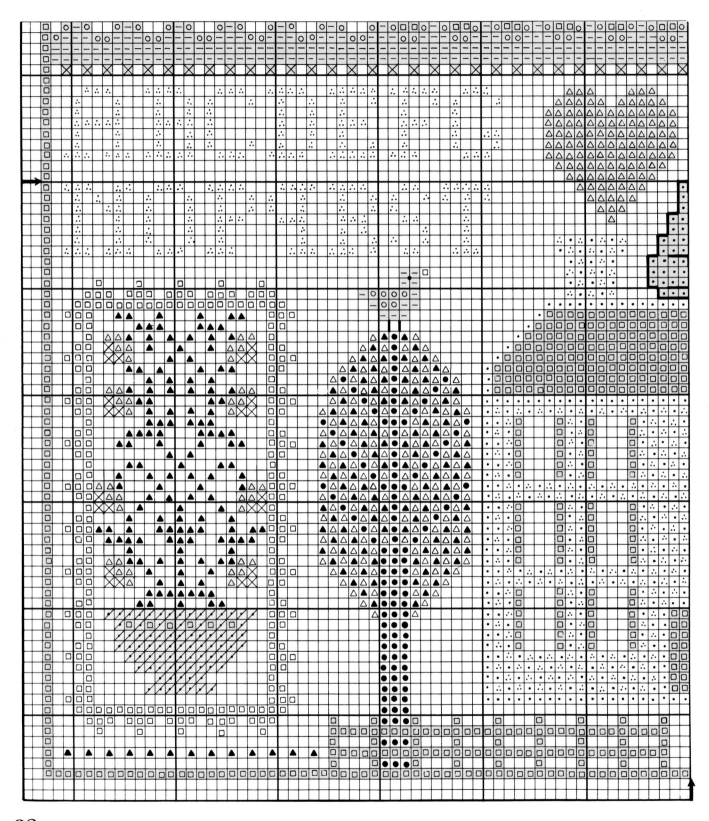

MALLARD MAT

Supplies

Completed design on Amaretto Murano 30
8¼" x 10¼" piece of mat board
Double-sided tape
Masking tape
Dressmaker's pen

Directions

1. To make window, cut a 3" x 4¼" rectangle in the center of the mat board.

2. With design piece centered, trim the Murano to measure 10¼" x 12¼".

3. Center the mat on the fabric and, with dressmaker's pen, trace the edge of the window onto the fabric. Then draw a smaller window 2" inside the first window. Cut along inside line. Clip the fabric at the corners almost to the edge of the mat.

4. On the wrong side of the mat, run a strip of double-sided tape around the edge of the window and around outside edge of mat. Fold the fabric over the mat edges, pulling it taut to fit. Secure with masking tape.

5. Place the mat in a ready-made frame or have a professional framer complete the framing.

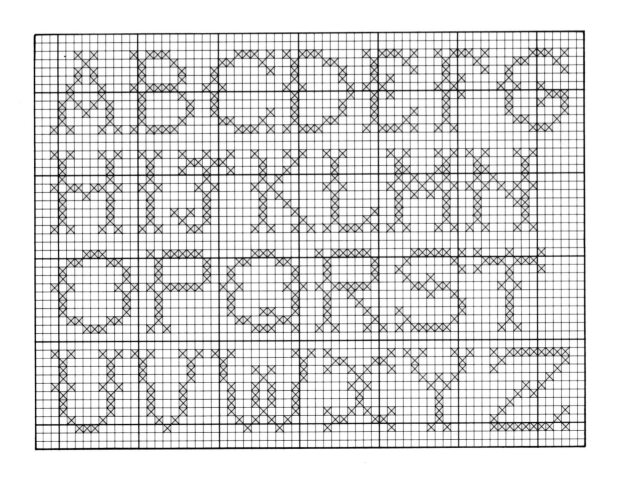

LIVING ROOMS

Stitched on Amaretto Murano 30 over two threads, the finished design size is 8⅜" x 6½". The fabric was cut 14" x 12".

FABRIC	DESIGN SIZE
Aida 11	11½" x 8⅞"
Aida 14	9" x 7"
Aida 18	7" x 5⅛"
Hardanger 22	5¾" x 4½"

Anchor   **DMC (used for sample)**

Step 1: Cross-stitch (2 strands)

Anchor			DMC	
387	·	/	712	Cream
901	□		680	Old Gold-dk.
338	∴	◢	3776	Mahogany-lt.
351	○	◔	400	Mahogany-dk.
341	✕	◸	919	Red Copper
922	∴	◢	930	Antique Blue-dk.
246	●	◔	319	Pistachio Green-vy. dk.
879	✕	◸	500	Blue Green-vy. dk.
956	ı	/	613	Drab Brown-lt.
898	△	◸	611	Drab Brown-dk.
914	■		3064	Pecan-lt.
236	✕	◸	3799	Pewter Gray-vy. dk.

Step 2: Backstitch (1 strand)

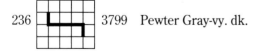

236	3799	Pewter Gray-vy. dk.

Step 3: French Knot (1 strand)

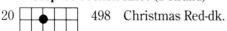

20	498	Christmas Red-dk.

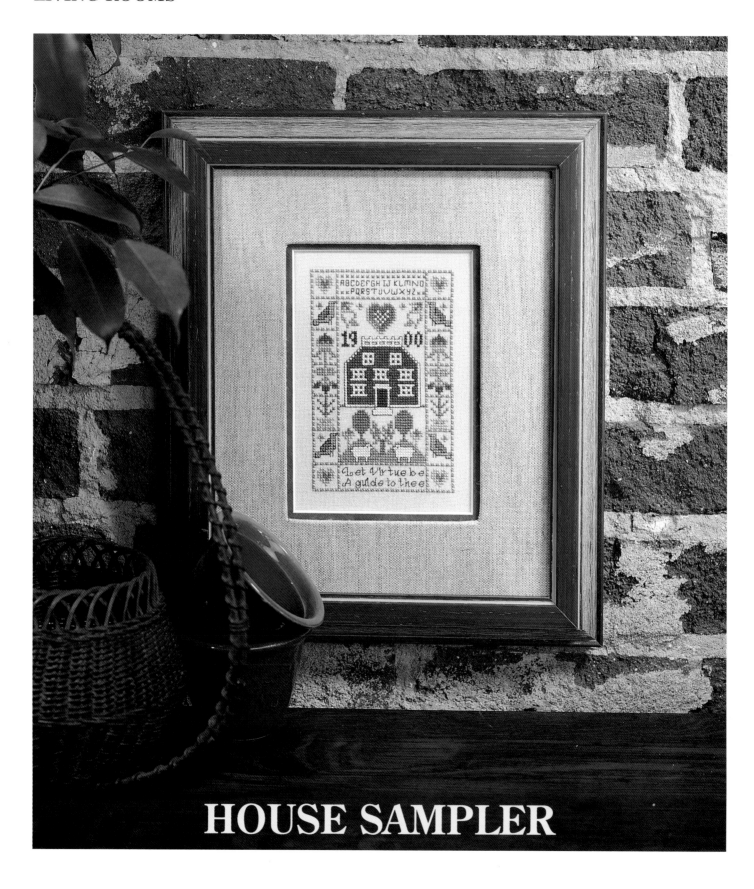

HOUSE SAMPLER

Stitched on Ivory Murano 30 over two threads, the finished design is 3¾" x 5⅝" for one repeat. The fabric was cut 10" x 12".

FABRIC	DESIGN SIZE
Aida 11	5⅛" x 7⅝"
Aida 14	4" x 6"
Aida 18	3⅛" x 4⅝"
Hardanger 22	2½" x 3⅞"

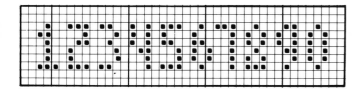

Anchor		DMC	(used for sample)

Step 1: Cross-stitch (2 strands)

Anchor		DMC	
387	·	712	Cream
868	ı	758	Terra Cotta-lt.
11	○	3328	Salmon-dk.
779	•	926	Slate Green
842	+	3013	Khaki Green-lt.
859	∴	3052	Green Gray-med.
878	▲	501	Blue Green-dk.
887	□	3046	Yellow Beige-med.
373	●	422	Hazel Nut Brown-lt.
375	⊠	420	Hazel Nut Brown-dk.
351	−	400	Mahogany-dk.
8581	⊠	3022	Brown Gray-med.
382	■	3021	Brown Gray-vy. dk.

Step 2: Backstitch (1 strand)

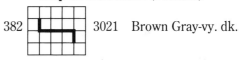

382		3021	Brown Gray-vy. dk.

Step 3: French Knot (1 strand)

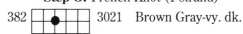

382	●	3021	Brown Gray-vy. dk.

Stitch Count: 56 x 84

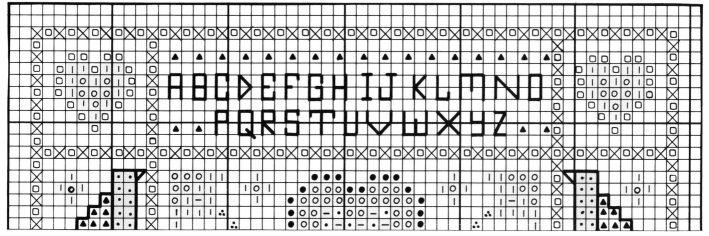

TRIMMED TREE

LIVING ROOMS

Stitched on Wedgewood Lugano 25 over two threads, the finished design is 9⅞" x 9". The fabric was cut 16" x 15". The tree is decorated with an Estaz (01) garland and 26 assorted brass/glass miniature Christmas ornaments.

FABRIC	DESIGN SIZE
Aida 11	11⅛" x 10⅛"
Aida 14	8¾" x 8"
Aida 18	6⅞" x 6¼"
Hardanger 22	5⅝" x 5⅛"

Stitch Count: 123 x 112

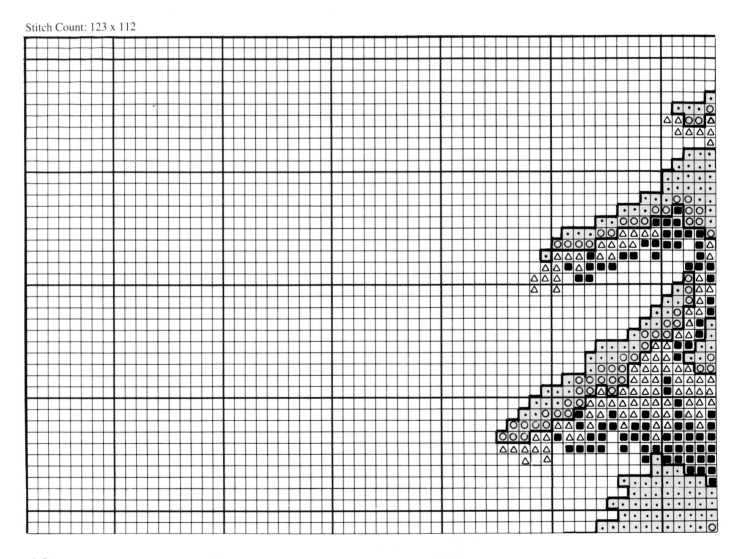

Anchor   **DMC (used for sample)**

Step 1: Cross-stitch (2 strands)

1	·	White
975	○	3753 Antique Blue-vy. lt.
210	△	562 Jade-med.
212	■	561 Jade-vy. dk.

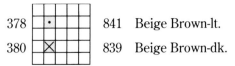

378	·	841 Beige Brown-lt.
380	⊠	839 Beige Brown-dk.

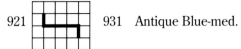

Step 2: Backstitch (1 strand)

921 931 Antique Blue-med.

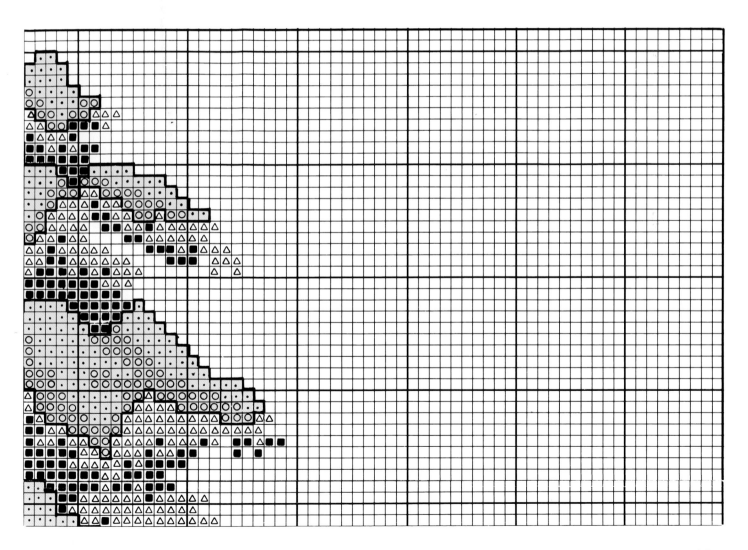

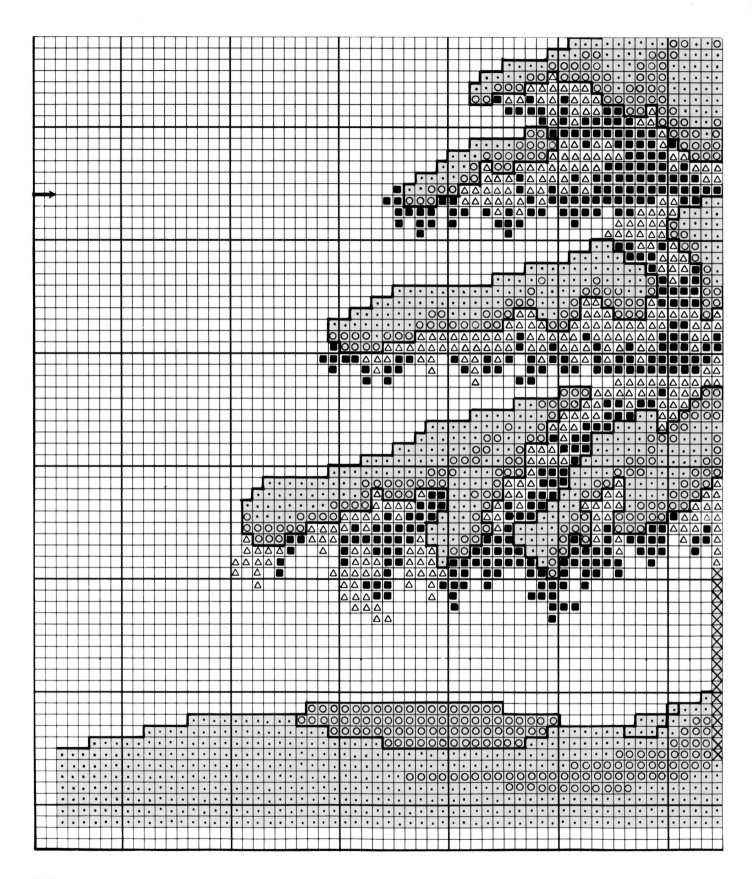

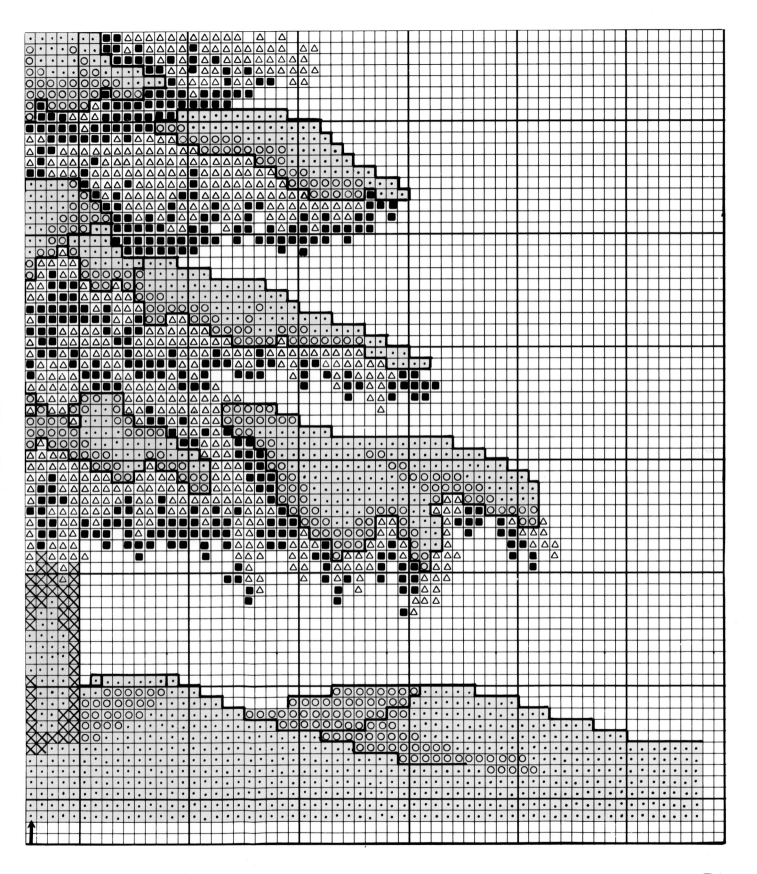

CHAPTER TWO

DINING ROOMS

CHECK   EMAT

Stitched on White Checkerboard Towel II 10 over one thread, the finished design is 1½" x 1½" for one repeat. The towel was cut in half and hemmed.

The napkin is made from a 15½" x 15½" piece of print fabric with matching thread. Hem, turning all edges under ½".

FABRIC	DESIGN SIZE
Aida 11	1⅜" x 1⅜"
Aida 14	1⅛" x 1⅛"
Aida 18	⅞" x ⅞"
Hardanger 22	⅝" x ⅝"

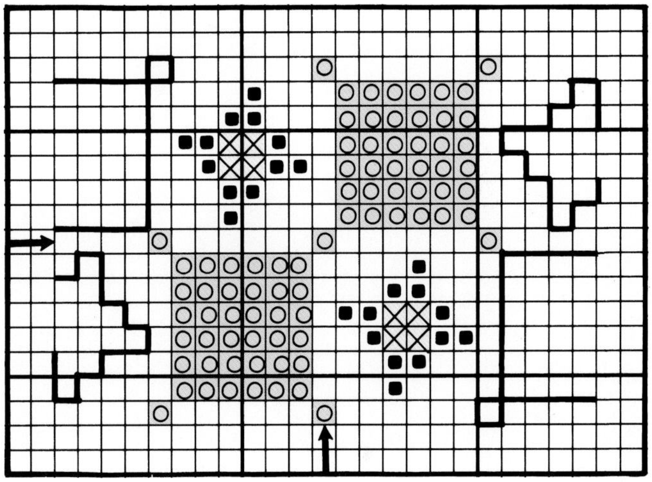

Anchor		DMC (used for sample)

Step 1: Cross-stitch (2 strands)

27	☒	899	Rose-med.
121	○	793	Cornflower Blue-med.
210	■	562	Jade-med.

Stitch Count: 15 x 15 for one repeat

FRUIT SACHET

Supplies

Completed design on Amaretto Murano 30;
   matching thread
5¾" x 13" piece of unstitched Amaretto Murano 30
1 yard of rayon cording
Potpourri

Directions

All seams are ¼".

1. With design centered, trim design piece to
5¾" x 13".

2. With right sides facing and raw edges aligned, stitch
front to back along side and bottom edges.

3. To make a boxed corners, at one bottom corner of
bag, align side and bottom seams by flattening bag.
With right sides facing and with one seam on top of
the other, finger-press seam allowances open. Stitch
across corner; see Diagram. Repeat for other bottom
corner. Clip corners; turn.

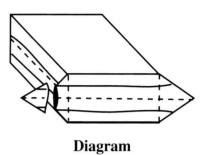

Diagram

4. Zigzag-stitch top edge. Fold top edge inward 3".
Press.

5. Stuff sachet moderately with potpourri. Knot ends
of rayon cording. Adjusting cording so that ends are
equal in length; tie a knot or bow to secure.

DINING ROOMS

Stitched on Amaretto Murano 30 over two threads, the finished design is 3⅜" x 3⅜". The fabric was cut 14" x 14".

FABRIC	DESIGN SIZE
Aida 11	4½" x 4½"
Aida 14	3⅝" x 3⅝"
Aida 18	2¾" x 2¾"
Hardanger 22	2¼" x 2¼"

Anchor   DMC (used for sample)

Step 1: Cross-stitch (2 strands)

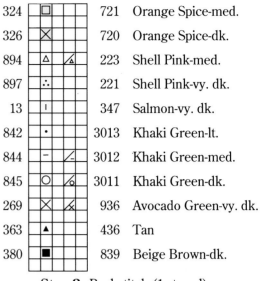

Anchor			DMC	
926				Ecru
886			677	Old Gold-vy. lt.
891			676	Old Gold-lt.
890			729	Old Gold-med.
323			722	Orange Spice-lt.
324			721	Orange Spice-med.
326			720	Orange Spice-dk.
894			223	Shell Pink-med.
897			221	Shell Pink-vy. dk.
13			347	Salmon-vy. dk.
842			3013	Khaki Green-lt.
844			3012	Khaki Green-med.
845			3011	Khaki Green-dk.
269			936	Avocado Green-vy. dk.
363			436	Tan
380			839	Beige Brown-dk.

Step 2: Backstitch (1 strand)

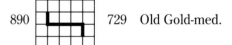

890		729	Old Gold-med.

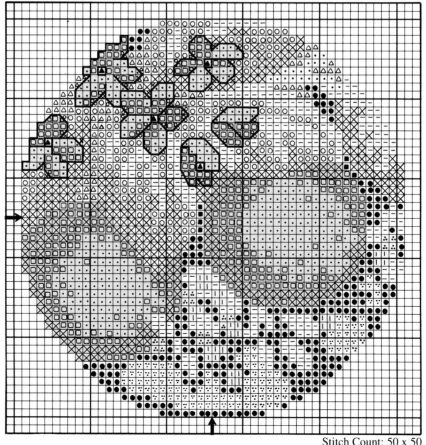

Stitch Count: 50 x 50

Stitched on Amaretto Murano 30 over two threads, the finished design is 3⅜" x 3⅜". The fabric was cut 14" x 14".

FABRIC	DESIGN SIZE
Aida 11	4½" x 4½"
Aida 14	3⅝" x 3⅝"
Aida 18	2¾" x 2¾"
Hardanger 22	2¼" x 2¼"

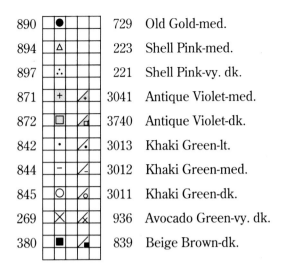

Anchor			DMC (used for sample)	
890	●		729	Old Gold-med.
894	△		223	Shell Pink-med.
897	∴		221	Shell Pink-vy. dk.
871	+	◿	3041	Antique Violet-med.
872	☐	◿	3740	Antique Violet-dk.
842	·	◿	3013	Khaki Green-lt.
844	−	◿	3012	Khaki Green-med.
845	○	◔	3011	Khaki Green-dk.
269	✕	◿	936	Avocado Green-vy. dk.
380	■	◿	839	Beige Brown-dk.

Step 1: Cross-stitch (2 strands)

Anchor			DMC	
926	·	◿		Ecru
300	I	◿	745	Yellow-lt. pale
886	☐	◿	677	Old Gold-vy. lt.
891	∴	◿	676	Old Gold-lt.

Step 2: Backstitch (1 strand)

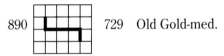

890		729	Old Gold-med.

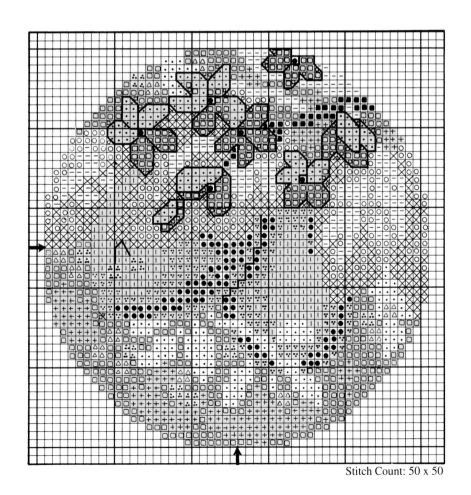

Stitch Count: 50 x 50

SERVING CLOTHS

Stitched on White Bread Cover 14 over one thread, the finished design is 3¼" x 2½". The design is centered diagonally in bottom right corner of fabric.

FABRIC	DESIGN SIZE
Aida 11	4⅛" x 3⅛"
Aida 14	3¼" x 2½"
Aida 18	2½" x 2"
Hardanger 22	2" x 1⅝"

Anchor   **DMC (used for sample)**

Step 1: Cross-stitch (2 strands)

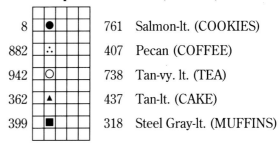

8	●	761	Salmon-lt. (COOKIES)
882	∴	407	Pecan (COFFEE)
942	○	738	Tan-vy. lt. (TEA)
362	▲	437	Tan-lt. (CAKE)
399	■	318	Steel Gray-lt. (MUFFINS)

Step 2: Backstitch (1 strand)

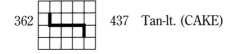

| 362 | | 437 | Tan-lt. (CAKE) |

Stitch Count: 45 x 35

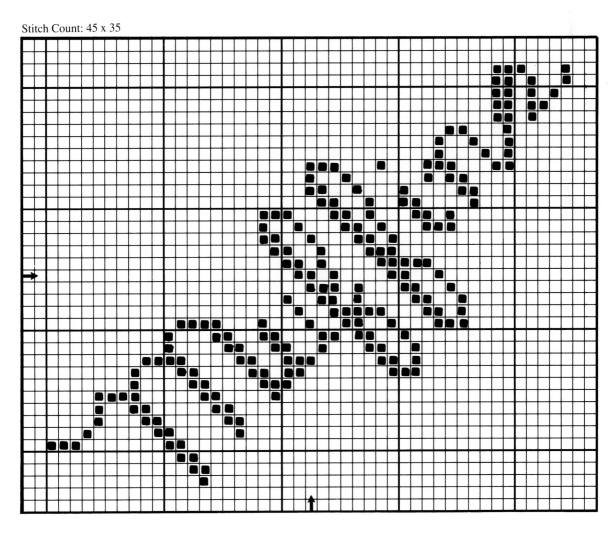

DINING ROOMS

Stitched on Cream Bread Cover 14 over one thread, the finished design is 2¾" x 2⅜". The design is centered diagonally in bottom right corner of fabric.

FABRIC	DESIGN SIZE
Aida 11	3½" x 3"
Aida 14	2¾" x 2⅜"
Aida 18	2⅛" x 1⅞"
Hardanger 22	1¾" x 1½"

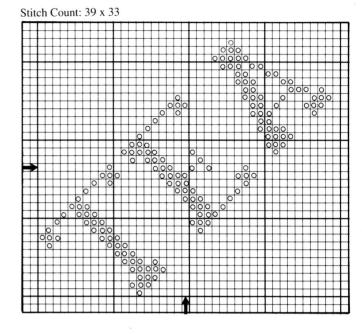

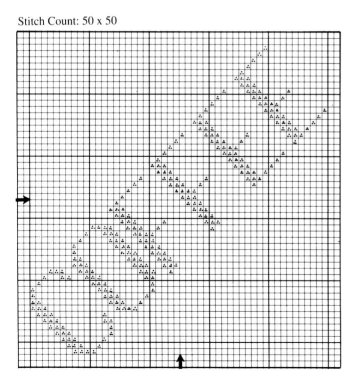

Stitched on Taupe Bread Cover 14 over one thread, the finished design is 3⅝" x 3⅝". The design is centered diagonally in top left corner of fabric.

FABRIC	DESIGN SIZE
Aida 11	4½" x 4½"
Aida 14	3⅝" x 3⅝"
Aida 18	2¾" x 2¾"
Hardanger 22	2¼" x 2¼"

Stitch Count: 36 x 31

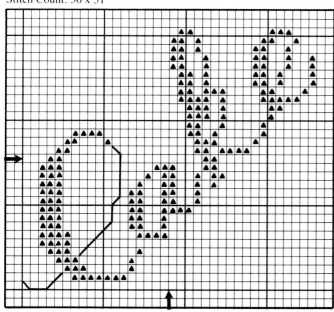

Stitched on Yellow Bread Cover 14 over one thread, the finished design is 2⅝" x 2¼". The design is centered diagonally in top left corner of fabric.

FABRIC	DESIGN SIZE
Aida 11	3¼" x 2⅞"
Aida 14	2⅝" x 2¼"
Aida 18	2" x 1¾"
Hardanger 22	1⅝" x 1⅜"

Stitched on Pink Bread Cover 14 over one thread, the finished design is 3⅛" x 3⅛". The design is centered diagonally in bottom right corner of fabric.

FABRIC	DESIGN SIZE
Aida 11	4" x 4"
Aida 14	3⅛" x 3⅛"
Aida 18	2½" x 2½"
Hardanger 22	2" x 2"

Stitch Count: 44 x 44

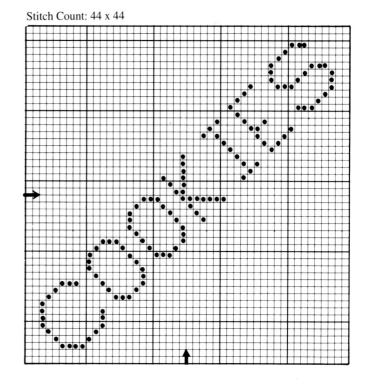

WINE BAG

Stitched on Amaretto Murano 30 over two threads, the finished design size is 1⅜" x 2⅝" for one repeat. The fabric was cut 16" x 18".

FABRIC	DESIGN SIZE
Aida 11	1⅞" x 3⅝"
Aida 14	1⅜" x 2⅞"
Aida 18	1⅛" x 2¼"
Hardanger 22	⅞" x 1⅞"

Supplies

Completed cross-stitch on Amaretto Murano 30;
   matching thread
½ yard of burgundy fabric; matching thread
¾ yard of ¼" burgundy cording
Wine bottle

Directions

All seams are ¼".

1. Trim design piece to 7" x 15" with design 3" from bottom, short edge. With wrong sides facing and design centered, fold Murano in half so that long edges meet. Stitch long edges to make a tube. Stitch bottom edge. Turn.

2. Cut one 7" x 15" piece from burgundy fabric for lining. With wrong sides facing, fold lining in half so that long edges meet. Stitch long edges. Stitch bottom edge, leaving an opening to turn.

3. Slide lining over Murano. Stitch top edge of lining to top edge of Murano. Turn lining through opening. Slipstitch opening closed. Place lining in bag. Knot ends of silk cording. Insert wine bottle into bag. Tie cording around bag at bottle neck.

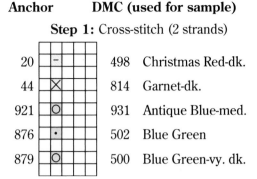

Anchor		DMC (used for sample)	
		**Step 1:** Cross-stitch (2 strands)	
20	−	498	Christmas Red-dk.
44	X	814	Garnet-dk.
921	O	931	Antique Blue-med.
876	·	502	Blue Green
879	O	500	Blue Green-vy. dk.

Stitch Count: 20 x 40 for one repeat

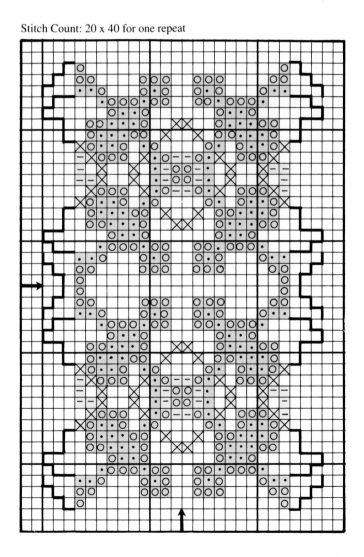

LEAF TABLE RUNNER

Supplies

Completed cross-stitch design on Cream Murano 30
1¾ yard of green leaf print fabric; matching thread
1⅛ yard of ⅜"-wide cream lace; matching thread

Directions

All seams are ¼".

1. With design centered, trim stitched design piece to
19½" x 3½". Trim green leaf print to 35" x 63".

2. Turn edges of design piece under. Center design
horizontally and 4½" from and parallel to one short
edge of green leaf fabric; topstitch on all edges. Cut
cream lace in half. Topstitch one length of lace just
above top edge of design piece. Repeat with remaining
length of lace, topstitching just below bottom edge of
design piece.

3. With right sides facing and long edges matching,
stitch long edges of green leaf fabric together. Press
flat with long seam centered at back. Stitch short
edges together, leaving an opening on one short seam.
Turn table runner through opening. Slipstitch opening.

Stitched on Cream Murano 30 over two threads, the
finished design size is 1¼" x 1⅞" for one repeat. The
fabric was cut 21" x 9".

FABRIC	DESIGN SIZE
Aida 11	1¾" x 2½"
Aida 14	1⅜" x 2"
Aida 18	1" x 1½"
Hardanger 22	5" x 1¼"

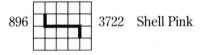

Anchor		DMC (used for sample)	

Step 1: Cross-stitch (2 strands)

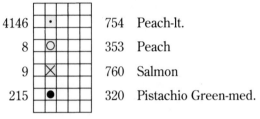

4146	·	754	Peach-lt.
8	O	353	Peach
9	X	760	Salmon
215	●	320	Pistachio Green-med.

Step 2: Backstitch (1 strand)

| 896 | | 3722 | Shell Pink |

Stitch Count: 19 x 28 for one repeat

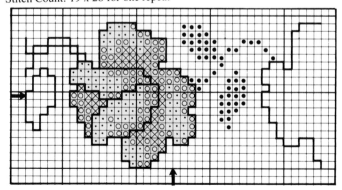

PEACH KITCHEN TOWEL

Stitched on Peach Nectar Kitchen Mates Towel 14 over one thread, the finished design is 3⅞" x 2" for one repeat. Heavy black lines on the graph indicate repeats. Begin stitching at center of towel and repeat design to fill length of towel.

FABRIC	DESIGN SIZE
Aida 11	5" x 2½"
Aida 14	3⅞" x 2"
Aida 18	3" x 1½"
Hardanger 22	2½" x 1¼"

Anchor   **DMC (used for sample)**

Step 1: Cross-stitch (2 strands)

Anchor		DMC	
10	⊠	352	Coral-lt.
11	○	350	Coral-med.
128	-	800	Delft-pale
878	■	501	Blue Green-dk.

Step 2: Backstitch (1 strand)

878		501	Blue Green-dk.

Stitch Count: 55 x 28 for one repeat

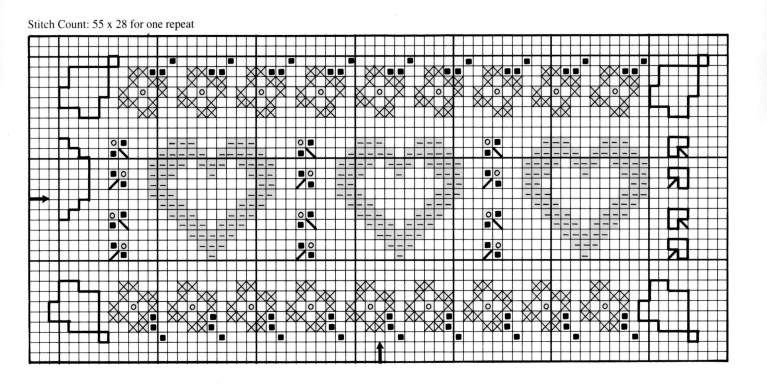

DELFT TEAPOTS

Stitched on White Jobelan 28 over two threads, the finished design is 5½" x 3½". The fabric was cut 12" x 10".

FABRIC   DESIGN SIZE
Aida 11   6⅞" x 4½"
Aida 14   5½" x 3½"
Aida 18   4¼" x 2¾"
Hardanger 22   3½" x 2¼"

Anchor   DMC (used for sample)

Step 1: Cross-stitch (2 strands)

975   3753   Antique Blue-vy. lt.
130   799   Delft-med.
941   791   Cornflower Blue-vy. dk.

Step 2: Backstitch (1 strand)

941   791   Cornflower Blue-vy. dk.

Stitch Count: 76 x 49

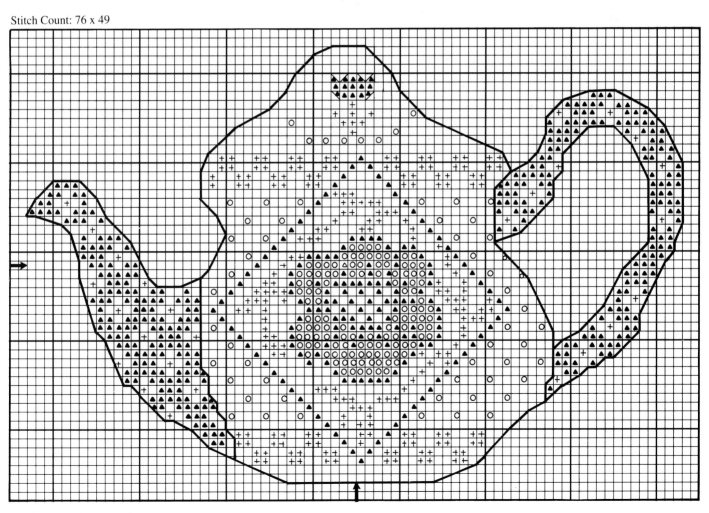

DINING ROOMS

Stitch Count: 69 x 51

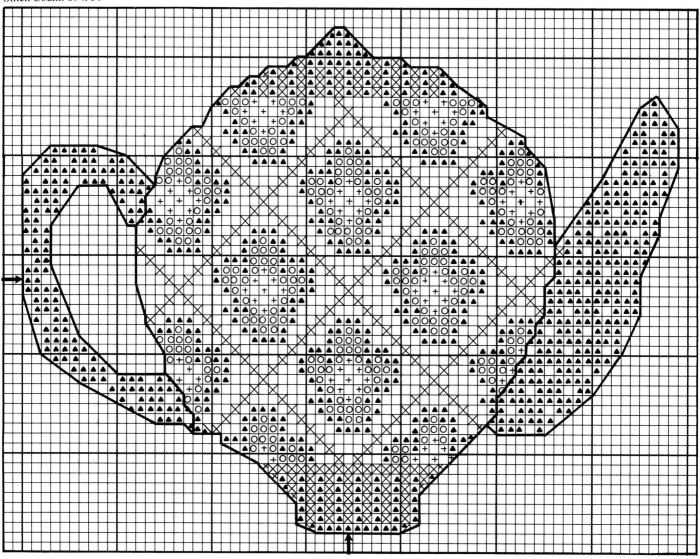

Stitched on White Jobelan 28 over two threads, the finished design is 4⅞" x 3⅝". The fabric was cut 11" x 10".

FABRIC	DESIGN SIZE
Aida 11	6¼" x 4⅝"
Aida 14	4⅞" x 3⅝"
Aida 18	3⅞" x 2⅞"
Hardanger 22	3⅛" x 2⅜"

Anchor   **DMC (used for sample)**

Step 1: Cross-stitch (2 strands)

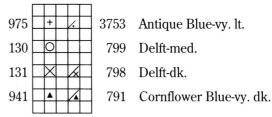

975	+	∕	3753	Antique Blue-vy. lt.
130	O		799	Delft-med.
131	X	✗	798	Delft-dk.
941	▲	◢	791	Cornflower Blue-vy. dk.

Step 2: Backstitch (1 strand)

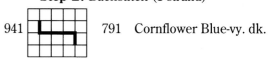

| 941 | ⌐ | 791 | Cornflower Blue-vy. dk. |

72

FARM ANIMAL SAMPLER

DINING ROOMS

Stitched on Linaida 14 over two threads, the finished design size is 6¼" x 6¼". The fabric was cut 13" x 13".

FABRIC	DESIGN SIZE
Aida 11	7⅞" x 7⅞"
Aida 14	6¼" x 6¼"
Aida 18	4⅞" x 4⅞"
Hardanger 22	4" x 4"

Stitch Count: 87 x 87

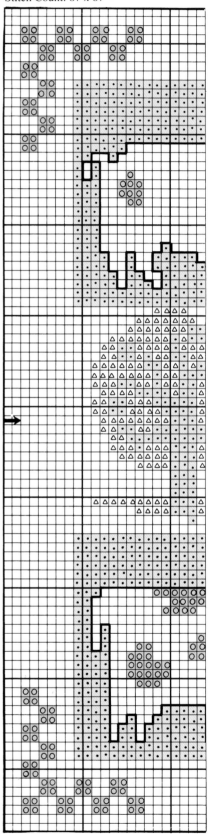

Anchor		DMC (used for sample)	

Step 1: Cross-stitch (2 strands)

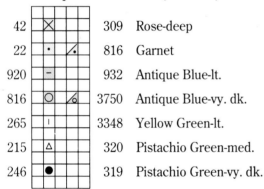

42	309	Rose-deep
22	816	Garnet
920	932	Antique Blue-lt.
816	3750	Antique Blue-vy. dk.
265	3348	Yellow Green-lt.
215	320	Pistachio Green-med.
246	319	Pistachio Green-vy. dk.

Step 2: Backstitch (1 strand)

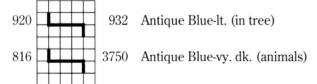

920	932	Antique Blue-lt. (in tree)
816	3750	Antique Blue-vy. dk. (animals)

74

CHAPTER THREE

Joys come from simple and natural things

BATHROOMS

PORCELAIN JARS

PORCELAIN JARS

Stitched on White Linen 36 over two threads, the
finished design size is 2⅝" x 2⅝". The fabric was cut
7" x 7". Insert design piece in jar lid, following
manufacturer's instructions.

FABRIC	DESIGN SIZE
Aida 11	4¼" x 4⅜"
Aida 14	3⅜" x 3⅜"
Aida 18	2⅝" x 2⅝"
Hardanger 22	2⅛" x 2⅛"

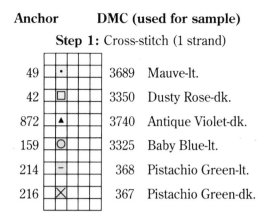

Anchor		DMC (used for sample)	
49	•	3689	Mauve-lt.
42	□	3350	Dusty Rose-dk.
872	▲	3740	Antique Violet-dk.
159	○	3325	Baby Blue-lt.
214	−	368	Pistachio Green-lt.
216	✕	367	Pistachio Green-dk.

Step 1: Cross-stitch (1 strand)

Stitch Count: 47 x 48

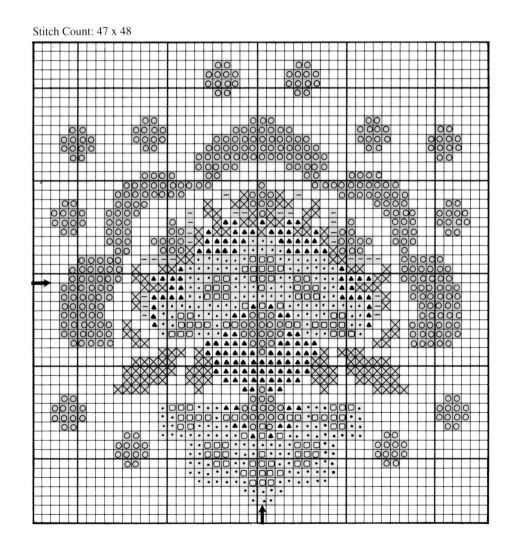

BATHROOMS

Stitched on White Linen 36 over two threads, the finished design size is 2⅝" x 2⅞". The fabric was cut 7" x 7". Insert design piece in jar lid, following manufacturer's instructions.

FABRIC	DESIGN SIZE
Aida 11	4⅜" x 4⅝"
Aida 14	3⅜" x 3⅝"
Aida 18	2⅝" x 2⅞"
Hardanger 22	2⅛" x 2⅜"

Anchor   **DMC (used for sample)**

Step 1: Cross-stitch (1 strand)

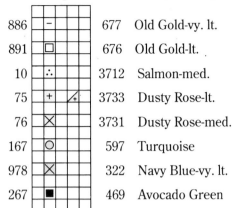

Anchor			DMC	
886	−		677	Old Gold-vy. lt.
891	□		676	Old Gold-lt.
10	∴		3712	Salmon-med.
75	+	⁄	3733	Dusty Rose-lt.
76	✕		3731	Dusty Rose-med.
167	○		597	Turquoise
978	✕		322	Navy Blue-vy. lt.
267	■		469	Avocado Green

Stitch Count: 48 x 51

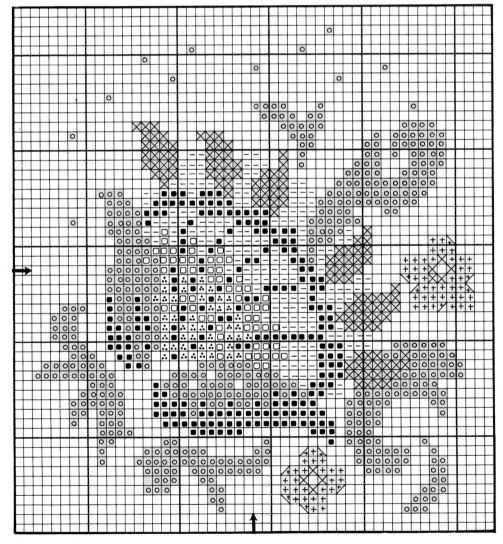

HAND TOWELS

BATHROOMS

Stitched on Ecru Kitchen Mates Towel 14 over one thread, the finished design is 6¼" x 2⅛" for one repeat. Heavy black lines on the graph indicate repeats. Begin stitching at center of towel and repeat design to fill length of towel.

FABRIC   DESIGN SIZE
Aida 11   7⅞" x 2⅝"
Aida 14   6¼" x 2⅛"
Aida 18   4⅞" x 1⅝"
Hardanger 22   4" x 1⅜"

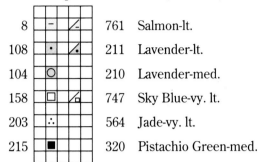

Anchor		DMC (used for sample)	

Step 1: Cross-stitch (2 strands)

		Anchor		DMC	
8			761	Salmon-lt.
108			211	Lavender-lt.
104			210	Lavender-med.
158			747	Sky Blue-vy. lt.
203			564	Jade-vy. lt.
215			320	Pistachio Green-med.

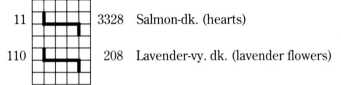

Step 2: Backstitch (1 strand)

11		3328	Salmon-dk. (hearts)
110		208	Lavender-vy. dk. (lavender flowers)

Stitch Count: 87 x 29 for one repeat

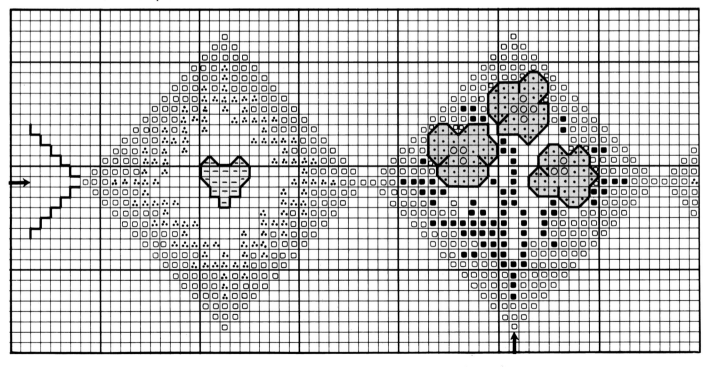

82

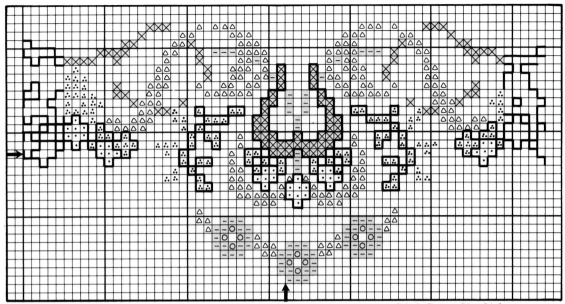

Stitch Count: 54 x 31 for one repeat

Stitched on Buttered Almond Kitchen Mates Towel 14 over one thread, the finished design is 3⅞" x 2¼" for one repeat. Heavy black lines on the graph indicate repeats. Begin stitching at center of towel and repeat design to fill length of towel.

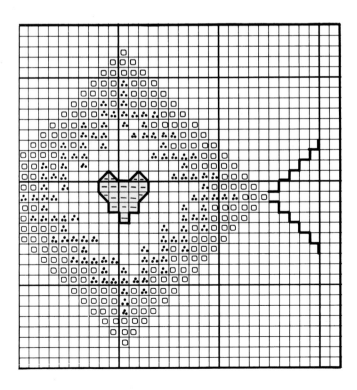

FABRIC	DESIGN SIZE
Aida 11	4⅞" x 2⅞"
Aida 14	3⅞" x 2¼"
Aida 18	3" x 1¾"
Hardanger 22	2½" x 1⅜"

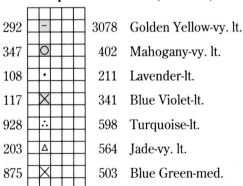

Anchor		DMC (used for sample)	
Step 1: Cross-stitch (2 strands)			
292	–	3078	Golden Yellow-vy. lt.
347	O	402	Mahogany-vy. lt.
108	•	211	Lavender-lt.
117	X	341	Blue Violet-lt.
928	∴	598	Turquoise-lt.
203	△	564	Jade-vy. lt.
875	X	503	Blue Green-med.
Step 2: Backstitch (1 strand)			
878		501	Blue Green-dk.

QUILT SQUARES

Stitched on Ivory Jobelan 28 over two threads, the finished design size is 2¼" x 2¼". The fabric was cut 9" x 9".

FABRIC	DESIGN SIZE
Aida 11	2⅞" x 2⅞"
Aida 14	2¼" x 2¼"
Aida 18	1¾" x 1¾"
Hardanger 22	1⅜" x 1⅜"

Anchor   **DMC (used for sample)**

Step 1: Cross-stitch (2 strands)

300	–	745	Yellow-lt. pale
338	O	3776	Mahogany-lt.
858	△	524	Fern Green-vy. lt.
859	▲	522	Fern Green

Floss Overdyed (2 strands)

| 187 | X | Island Shores |

Stitch Count: 31 x 31

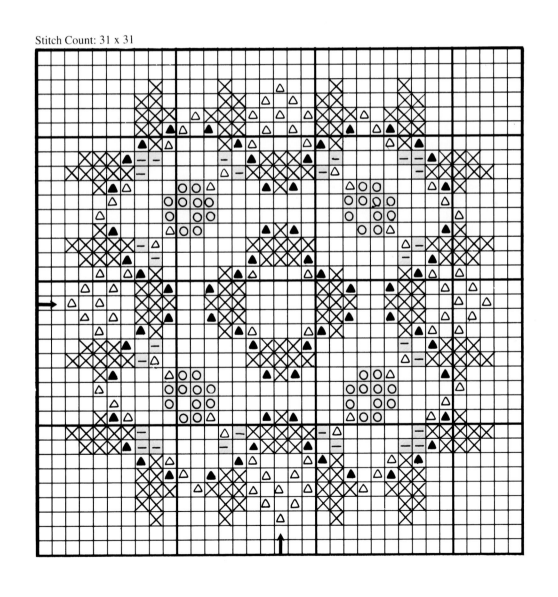

BATHROOMS

Stitched on Ivory Jobelan 28 over two threads, the finished design size is 2¼" x 2¼". The fabric was cut 9" x 9".

FABRIC	DESIGN SIZE
Aida 11	2⅞" x 2⅞"
Aida 14	2¼" x 2¼"
Aida 18	1¾" x 1¾"
Hardanger 22	1⅜" x 1⅜"

Anchor		DMC (used for sample)	
Step 1: Cross-stitch (2 strands)			
862	∴	3362	Pine Green-dk.
373	☐	422	Hazel Nut Brown-lt.
Floss Overdyed (2 strands)			
	△	130	Woodland Fantasy

Stitch Count: 31 x 31

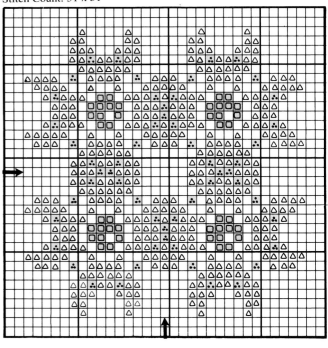

Stitch Count: 31 x 31

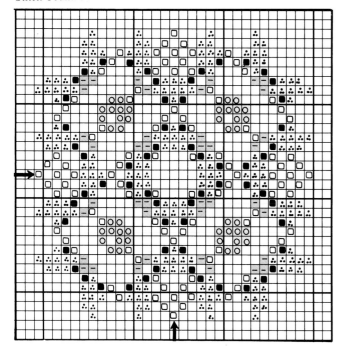

Stitched on Ivory Jobelan 28 over two threads, the finished design size is 2¼" x 2¼". The fabric was cut 9" x 9".

FABRIC	DESIGN SIZE
Aida 11	2⅞" x 2⅞"
Aida 14	2¼" x 2¼"
Aida 18	1¾" x 1¾"
Hardanger 22	1⅜" x 1⅜"

Anchor		DMC (used for sample)	
Step 1: Cross-stitch (2 strands)			
300	–	745	Yellow-lt. pale
4146	O	754	Peach-lt.
843	☐	3364	Pine Green
861	■	3363	Pine Green-med.
Floss Overdyed (2 strands)			
	∴	123	Bear Brown

BATHROOMS

Stitched on Rustico Aida 18 over one thread, the finished design size is 6⅛" x 1½" for one repeat. Heavy black lines on the graph indicate repeats. Begin stitching at center of fabric and repeat design to fill desired length. The fabric was cut 18" x 6".

FABRIC	DESIGN SIZE
Aida 11	10⅛" x 2½"
Aida 14	7⅞" x 1⅞"
Hardanger 22	5" x 1¼"

Anchor		DMC (used for sample)	
Step 1: Cross-stitch (2 strands)			
373	□	3045	Yellow Beige-dk.
4146	·	754	Peach-lt.
9	−	760	Salmon
894	O	223	Shell Pink-med.
860		3053	Green Gray
846	X	3051	Green Gray-dk.
Step 2: Backstitch (1 strand)			
896		3722	Shell Pink

Stitch Count: 111 x 27 for one repeat

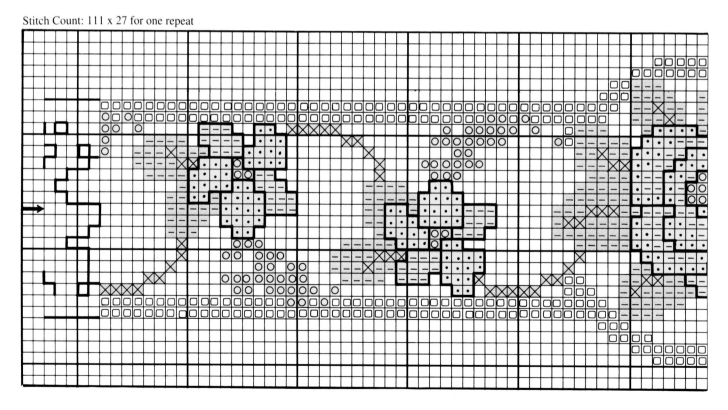

Supplies

Completed design piece on Rustico Aida 18;
  matching thread
⅛ yard of pink satin; matching thread
Package of scented soaps

Directions

All seams are ¼".

1. Center design and trim long edges to ⅝" above and below stitched border. Measure around soap package, trim ends of design piece to match measurement, adding ½" on each end. From pink satin, cut piece to match size of trimmed design piece.

2. With right sides together, stitch long edges of satin and design piece together. Turn. Center design; fold and press. Turn inside ¼" unstitched fabric at one short end; pin. Tuck opposite short end of design piece in so soap band fits snugly around package. Slipstitch ends. Slide band onto soap package.

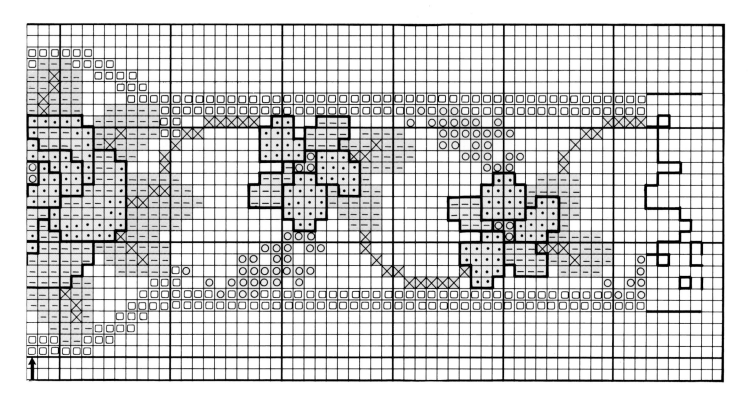

BATHROOMS

Supplies

Completed design piece on Cream Aida 18;
   matching thread
Package of scented soaps

Directions

All seams are ¼".

1. Center design and trim long edges to 2" above and below widest point of design. Measure around soap package; trim ends of design piece to match measurement, adding ½" on each end.

2. With right sides facing and long edges matching, stitch together at long edge. Turn. Center design; fold and press.

3. Turn inside ¼" unstitched fabric at one short end; pin. Tuck opposite short end of design piece in so soap band fits snugly around package. Slipstitch ends. Slide band onto soap package.

Stitched on Cream Aida 18 over one thread, the finished design size is 3⅜" x 2¼" for one repeat. Heavy black lines on the graph indicate repeats. Begin stitching at center of fabric and repeat design to fill desired length. The fabric was cut 16" x 7".

FABRIC	DESIGN SIZE
Aida 11	5½" x 3¾"
Aida 14	4¼" x 2⅞"
Hardanger 22	2¾" x 1⅞"

Anchor   DMC (used for sample)

Step 1: Cross-stitch (2 strands)

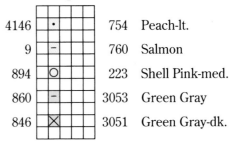

4146	•	754	Peach-lt.
9	–	760	Salmon
894	O	223	Shell Pink-med.
860	–	3053	Green Gray
846	X	3051	Green Gray-dk.

Step 2: Backstitch (1 strand)

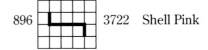

| 896 | | 3722 | Shell Pink |

Stitch Count: 60 x 41 for one repeat

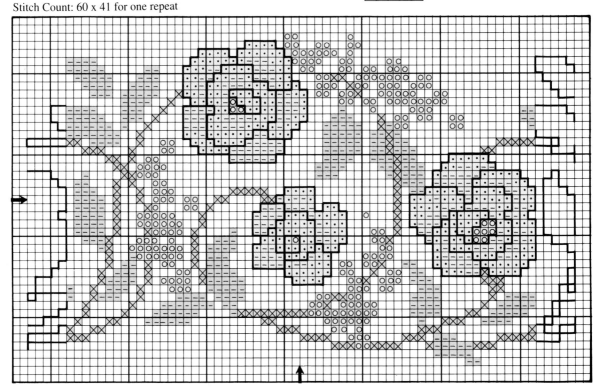

PANSY PASSION

BATHROOMS

Stitch Count: 84 x 70

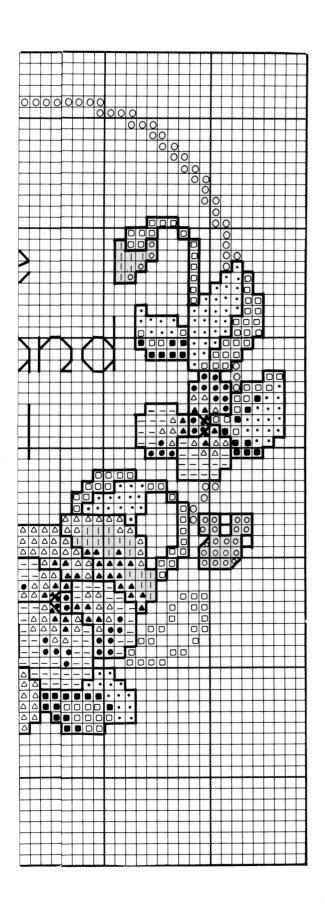

Stitched on White Belfast Linen 32 over two threads, the finished design size is 5¼" x 4⅜". The fabric was cut 12" x 11".

FABRIC	DESIGN SIZE
Aida 11	7⅝" x 6⅜"
Aida 14	6" x 5"
Aida 18	4⅝" x 3⅞"
Hardanger 22	3⅞" x 3⅛"

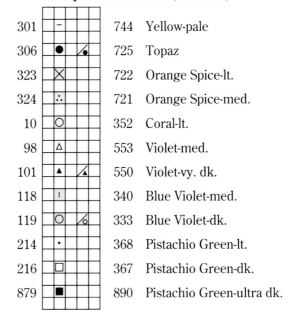

Anchor   **DMC (used for sample)**

Step 1: Cross-stitch (2 strands)

Anchor			DMC	
301	–		744	Yellow-pale
306	●	⟋•	725	Topaz
323	✕		722	Orange Spice-lt.
324	∴		721	Orange Spice-med.
10	○		352	Coral-lt.
98	△		553	Violet-med.
101	▲	⟋	550	Violet-vy. dk.
118	I		340	Blue Violet-med.
119	⊙	⟋	333	Blue Violet-dk.
214	•		368	Pistachio Green-lt.
216	☐		367	Pistachio Green-dk.
879	■		890	Pistachio Green-ultra dk.

Step 2: Backstitch (1 strand)

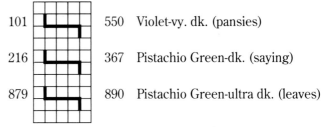

	DMC	
101	550	Violet-vy. dk. (pansies)
216	367	Pistachio Green-dk. (saying)
879	890	Pistachio Green-ultra dk. (leaves)

Step 3: French Knot (1 strand)

216	●	367	Pistachio Green-dk.

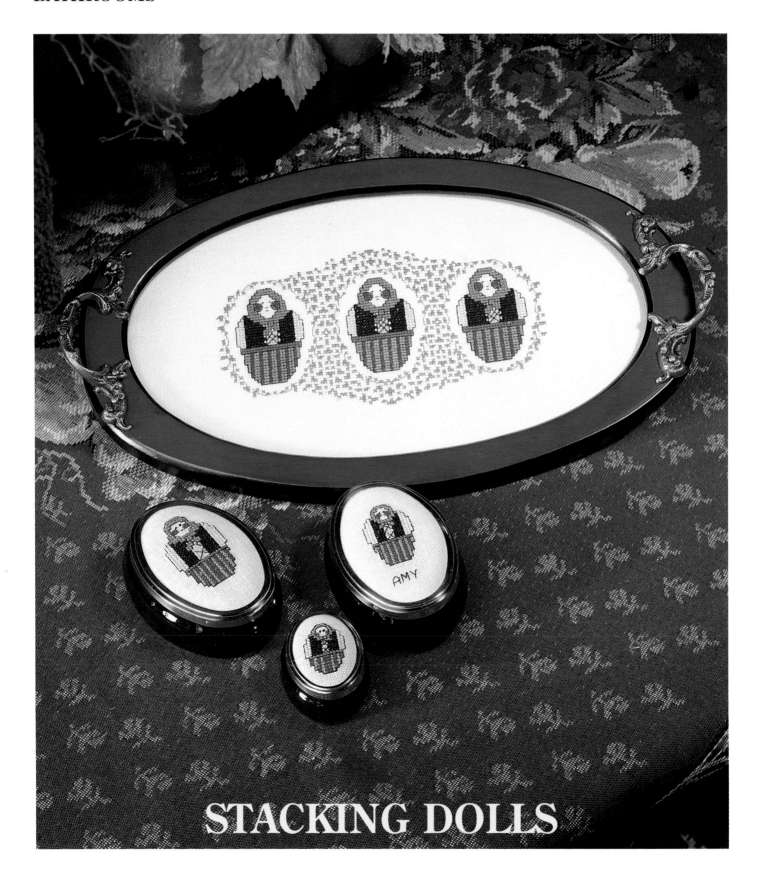

STACKING DOLLS

Stitched on Cream Belfast Linen 32 over two threads, the finished design size is 1⅛" x 1¾". The fabric was cut 6" x 6". Insert design piece in lid, following manufacturer's instructions.

Stitched on Cream Belfast Linen 32 over two threads, the finished design size is 1" x 1⅞". The fabric was cut 6" x 6". Insert design piece in lid, following manufacturer's instructions.

FABRIC	DESIGN SIZE
Aida 11	1⅝" x 2⅝"
Aida 14	1¼" x 2⅛"
Aida 18	1" x 1⅝"
Hardanger 22	⅞" x 1⅜"

FABRIC	DESIGN SIZE
Aida 11	1⅜" x 2¾"
Aida 14	1⅛" x 2⅛"
Aida 18	⅞" x 1⅝"
Hardanger 22	⅝" x 1⅜"

Stitch Count: 18 x 29

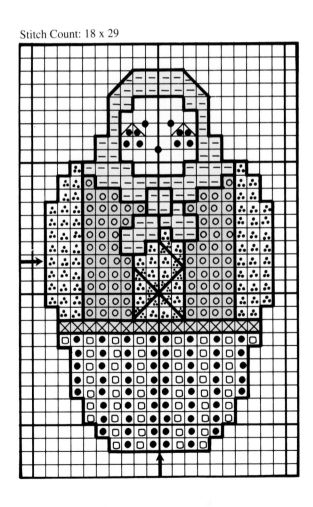

Stitch Count: 15 x 30

BATHROOMS

Stitched on Cream Belfast Linen 32 over two threads, the finished design size is ¾" x 1⅛". The fabric was cut 4" x 4". Insert design piece in lid, following manufacturer's instructions.

FABRIC	DESIGN SIZE
Aida 11	1⅛" x 1⅝"
Aida 14	⅞" x 1¼"
Aida 18	⅝" x 1"
Hardanger 22	½" x ⅞"

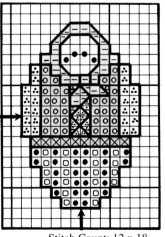

Stitch Count: 12 x 18

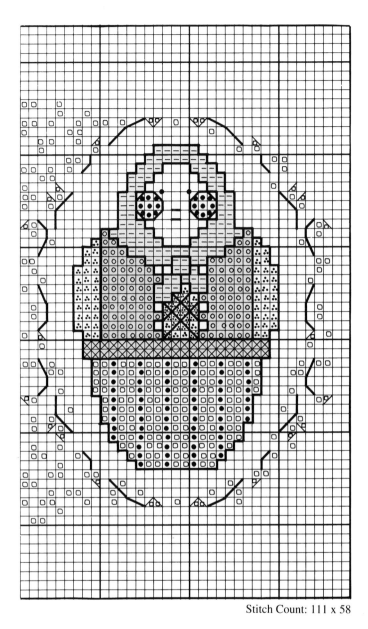

Stitch Count: 111 x 58

Stitched on Cream Belfast Linen 32 over two threads, the finished design size is 7" x 3⅝". The fabric was cut 13" x 10". Insert design piece in tray, following manufacturer's instructions.

FABRIC	DESIGN SIZE
Aida 11	10⅛" x 5¼"
Aida 14	7⅞" x 4⅛"
Aida 18	6⅛" x 3¼"
Hardanger 22	5" x 2⅝"

Anchor		DMC (used for sample)	
Step 1: Cross-stitch (2 strands)			
891		676	Old Gold-lt.
11		3328	Salmon-dk.
19		817	Coral Red-vy. dk.
101		327	Antique Violet-vy. dk.
216		367	Pistachio Green-dk.
403		310	Black
Step 2: Backstitch (1 strand)			
216		367	Pistachio Green-dk. (ivy)
403		310	Black (dolls)
Step 3: French Knot (1 strand)			
403		310	Black

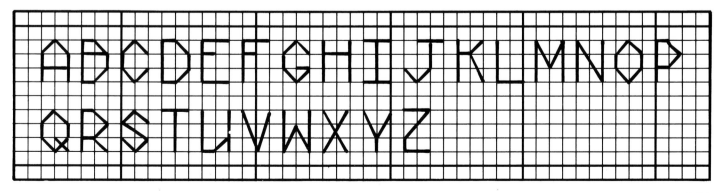

CRYSTAL JAR

Stitched on White Belfast Linen 32 over two threads, the finished design size is 2¼" x 2¼". The fabric was cut 6" x 6". Insert design piece in jar lid, following manufacturer's instructions.

FABRIC	DESIGN SIZE
Aida 11	3⅛" x 3⅛"
Aida 14	2½" x 2½"
Aida 18	2" x 2"
Hardanger 22	1⅝" x 1⅝"

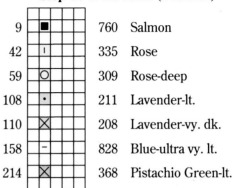

Anchor		DMC (used for sample)	
Step 1: Cross-stitch (2 strands)			
9	■	760	Salmon
42	ı	335	Rose
59	O	309	Rose-deep
108	•	211	Lavender-lt.
110	X	208	Lavender-vy. dk.
158	–	828	Blue-ultra vy. lt.
214	X	368	Pistachio Green-lt.

Stitch Count: 35 x 35

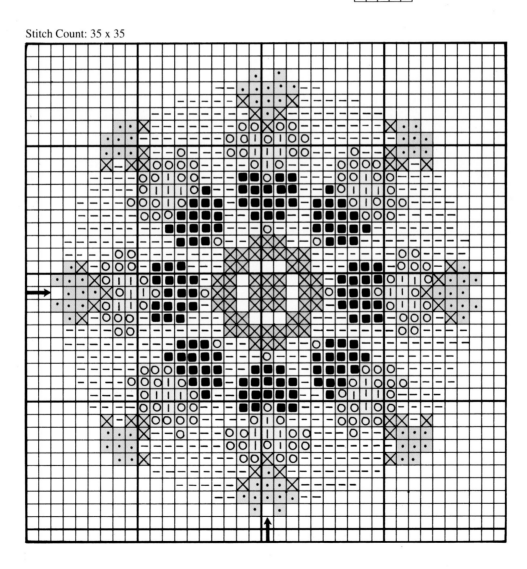

ROSY BATH TOWEL

Stitched on White Terry Bath Towel 14 over one thread, the finished design size is 5½" x 2¾" for one motif. Heavy black lines on the graph indicate repeats. Begin stitching at center of towel and repeat design to fill width of towel.

FABRIC	DESIGN SIZE
Aida 11	7" x 3½"
Aida 14	5½" x 2¾"
Aida 18	4¼" x 2⅛"
Hardanger 22	3½" x 1¾"

Anchor		DMC (used for sample)	
Step 1: Cross-stitch (2 strands)			
75	○	3733	Dusty Rose-lt.
76	✕	3731	Dusty Rose-med.
859	■	522	Fern Green

Stitch Count: 77 x 38 for one motif

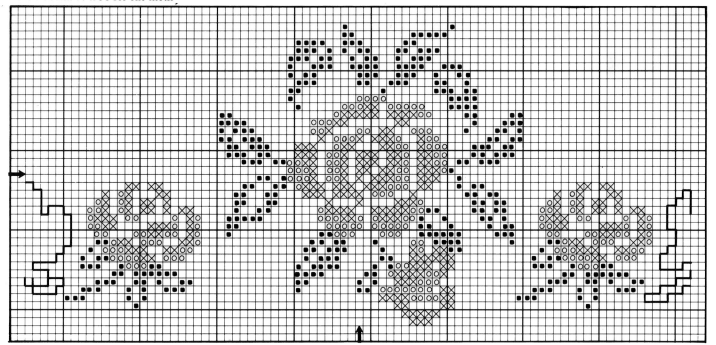

CHAPTER FOUR

BEDROOMS

LITTLE BO PEEP

Supplies

Completed design on White Belfast Linen 32;
   matching thread
4 yards of 1"-wide white scalloped lace trim
Dressmaker's pen

Directions

1. Do not trim design piece. Zigzag edges. To hem
fabric, turn long edges under ½". Press and baste.
Using dressmaker's pen, mark trim lines on short edge
below stitched area; see Diagram. Trim edge. Repeat
on opposite short edge. Turn both edges under ½",
mitering corners. Press and baste.

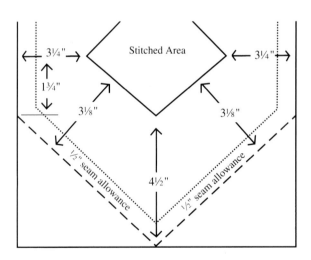

Diagram

2. Stitch hem in place, pressing again if necessary.
Remove basting.

3. To finish table runner, stitch lace trim along edges
of design piece, gathering lace slightly to fit corners.

Stitched on White Belfast Linen 32 over two threads,
the finished design size is 5¼" x 5". The fabric was
cut 54" x 12". Begin stitching with design centered
horizontally and bottom point of design 4½" from one
short edge of fabric; see Step 1 of directions.

FABRIC	DESIGN SIZE
Aida 11	7⅝" x 7⅜"
Aida 14	6" x 5¾"
Aida 18	4⅝" x 4½"
Hardanger 22	3⅞" x 3⅝"

Anchor		DMC (used for sample)

Step 1: Cross-stitch (2 strands)

75   3733   Dusty Rose-lt.

Step 2: Backstitch (1 strand)

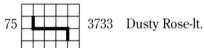

75   3733   Dusty Rose-lt.

BEDROOMS

Stitch Count: 84 x 81

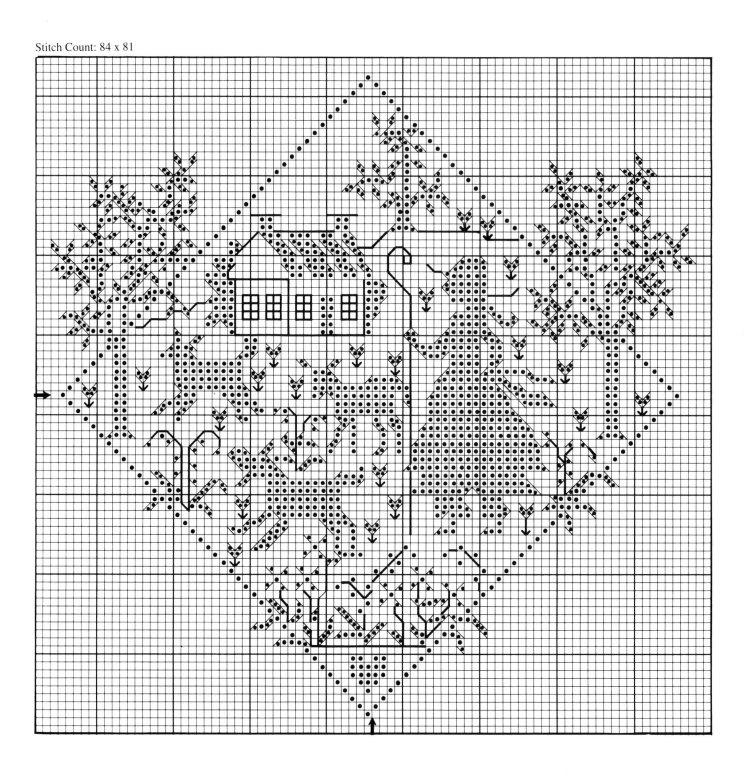

JACK-IN-THE-BOX

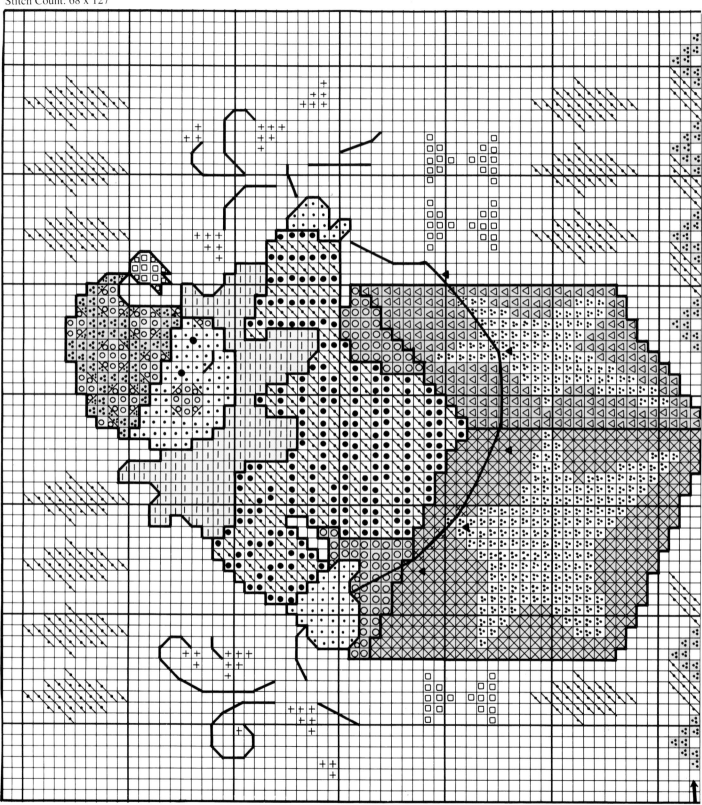

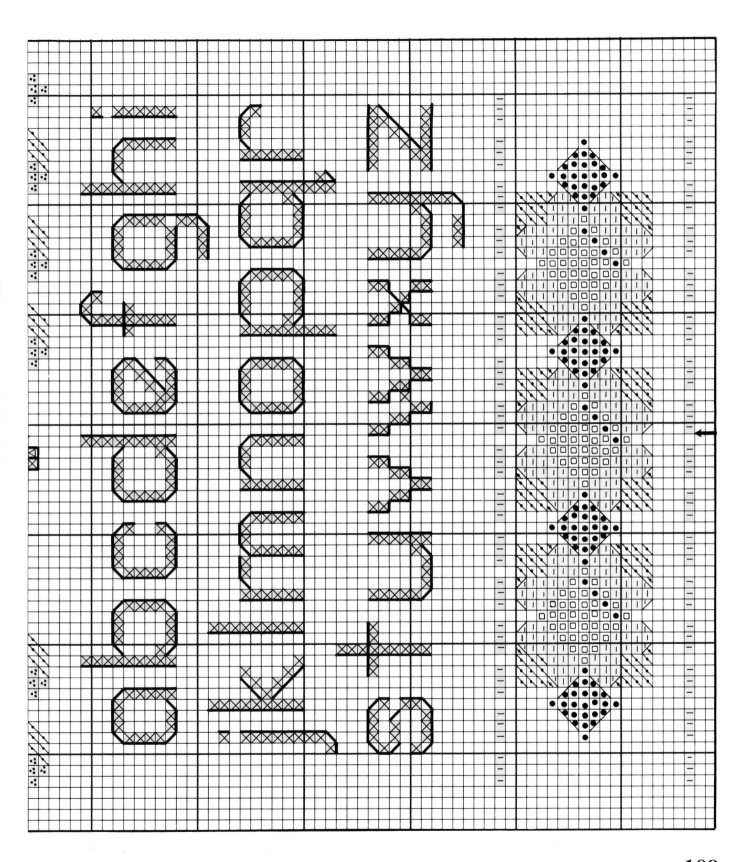

109

BEDROOMS

Stitched on Yellow Aida 14 over one thread, the finished design size is 4⅞" x 9⅛". The fabric was cut 11" x 16".

FABRIC	DESIGN SIZE
Aida 11	6⅛" x 11½"
Aida 18	3¾" x 7"
Hardanger 22	3⅛" x 5¾"

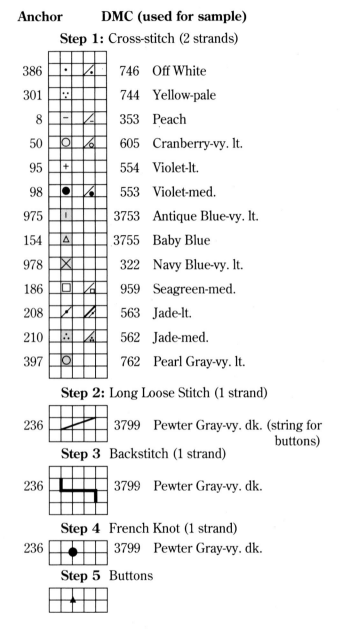

Anchor   **DMC (used for sample)**

Step 1: Cross-stitch (2 strands)

386	746	Off White
301	744	Yellow-pale
8	353	Peach
50	605	Cranberry-vy. lt.
95	554	Violet-lt.
98	553	Violet-med.
975	3753	Antique Blue-vy. lt.
154	3755	Baby Blue
978	322	Navy Blue-vy. lt.
186	959	Seagreen-med.
208	563	Jade-lt.
210	562	Jade-med.
397	762	Pearl Gray-vy. lt.

Step 2: Long Loose Stitch (1 strand)

| 236 | 3799 | Pewter Gray-vy. dk. (string for buttons) |

Step 3 Backstitch (1 strand)

| 236 | 3799 | Pewter Gray-vy. dk. |

Step 4 French Knot (1 strand)

| 236 | 3799 | Pewter Gray-vy. dk. |

Step 5 Buttons

BEDROOMS

Stitched on Floba 18 over two threads, the finished design size is 4½" x 2¼". The fabric was cut 10" x 10".

FABRIC	DESIGN SIZE
Aida 11	3½" x 1⅞"
Aida 14	2¾" x 1⅜"
Aida 18	2⅛" x 1⅛"
Hardanger 22	1¾" x ⅞"

Anchor   DMC (used for sample)

Step 1: Cross-stitch (2 strands)

Anchor		DMC	
868	–	758	Terra Cotta-lt.
5975	X	356	Terra Cotta-med.
779	O	926	Slate Green
214	I	368	Pistachio Green-lt.
215	□	320	Pistachio Green-med.
246	■	319	Pistachio Green-vy. dk.

Supplies

Completed design on Floba 18; matching thread
5½" x 10" piece of unstitched Floba 18 for back
¼ yard of green fabric; matching thread
Fragrant pine needles

Directions

1. With design centered, trim design piece to 5½" x 10" for front. From green fabric, cut one 9¼" x 9" piece.

2. With right sides facing and raw edges aligned, stitch front design to unstitched back along side and bottom edges. Zigzag-stitch top edge. Fold top edges inward 3". Press.

3. To make pillow, fold green fabric in half with right sides facing and short ends matching; stitch along side and bottom edges, leaving a small opening. Stuff firmly with pine needles. Slipstitch opening closed. Place pillow inside sleeve.

Stitch Count: 38 x 20

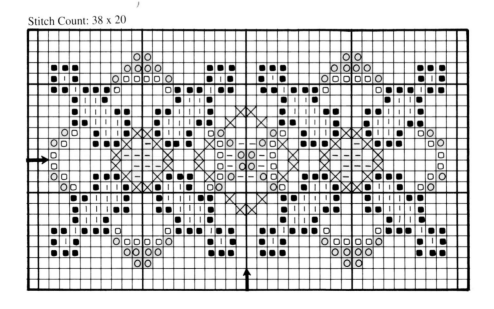

BABY'S BOMBER BLANKET

BEDROOMS

Stitched on Soft Touch Blankie 14 over one thread, the finished design size is 2⅝" x 1¾" for one motif. The blanket size is 30" x 36". Heavy black lines on the graph indicate repeats. Begin stitching first motif in one corner of blanket with bottom of design 2" from blanket binding.

FABRIC	DESIGN SIZE
Aida 11	3⅜" x 2¼"
Aida 14	2⅝" x 1¾"
Aida 18	2" x 1⅜"
Hardanger 22	1⅝" x 1⅛"

Stitch Count: 37 x 25

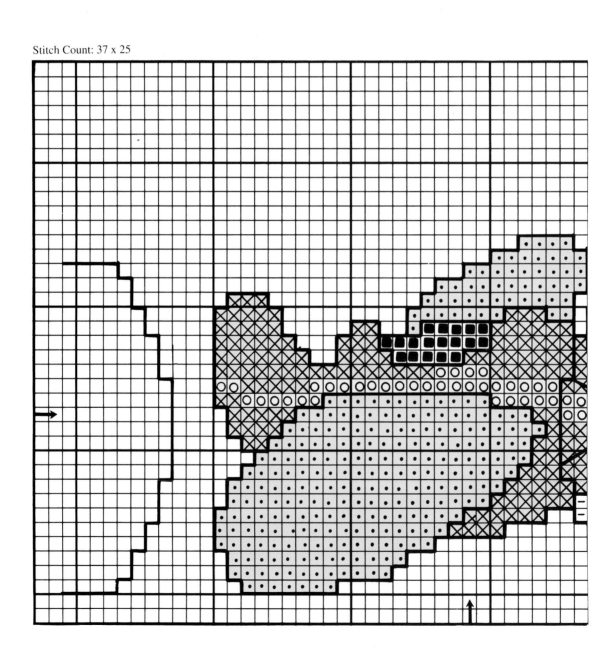

Anchor   **DMC (used for sample)**

Step 1: Cross-stitch (2 strands)

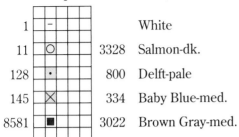

1	—	White
11	○	3328 Salmon-dk.
128	·	800 Delft-pale
145	✕	334 Baby Blue-med.
8581	■	3022 Brown Gray-med.

Step 2: Long Loose Stitch (1 strand)

236   3799   Pewter Gray-vy. dk. (in propeller)

Step 3: Backstitch (1 strand)

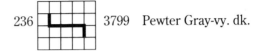

236   3799   Pewter Gray-vy. dk.

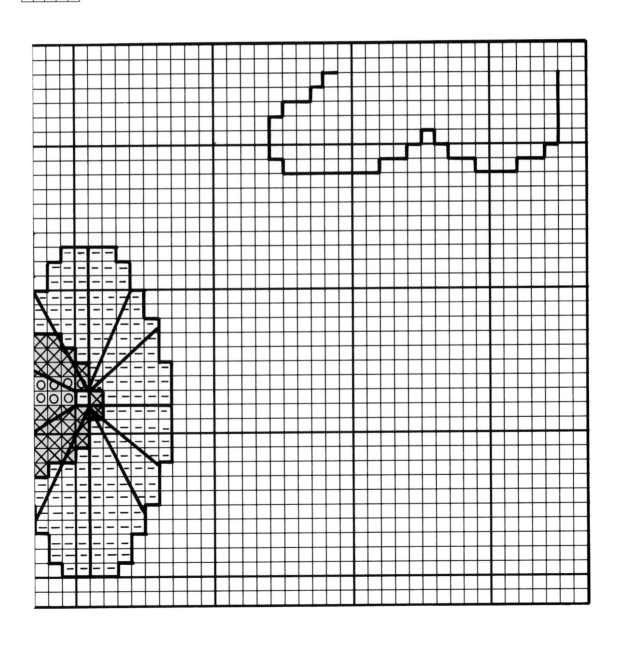

BABY'S SLEEPING

Supplies

Completed design on Yellow Aida 14
6" x 8" of unstitched Yellow Aida 14;
  matching thread
⅛ yard of blue fabric
¾ yard of narrow cording
2 yards of ½"-wide blue satin ribbon
Stuffing

Directions

All seams are ¼".

1. With design centered, trim stitched design piece to 6" x 8". From blue fabric, cut 1½"-wide bias strips, piecing as needed to equal ¾ yard. Make piping.

2. With right sides facing and raw edges aligned, stitch piping around all edges of pillow front. With right sides facing, stitch pillow front to pillow back, sewing along stitching line of piping and leaving an opening on one edge. Trim corners and turn. Stuff moderately with stuffing and slipstitch opening closed.

3. From blue ribbon, cut two 19" lengths, two 5" lengths and one 24" length. With small stitches, tack one end of one 19" length to one top corner of pillow. Repeat with remaining 19" length.

4. Tie 5" lengths in two small bows. Tack to top pillow corners, covering raw ribbon ends. Knot free ribbon ends together, leaving 10" tails. Handling tails and remaining ribbon length as one, tie a bow.

BEDROOMS

Stitch Count: 71 x 99

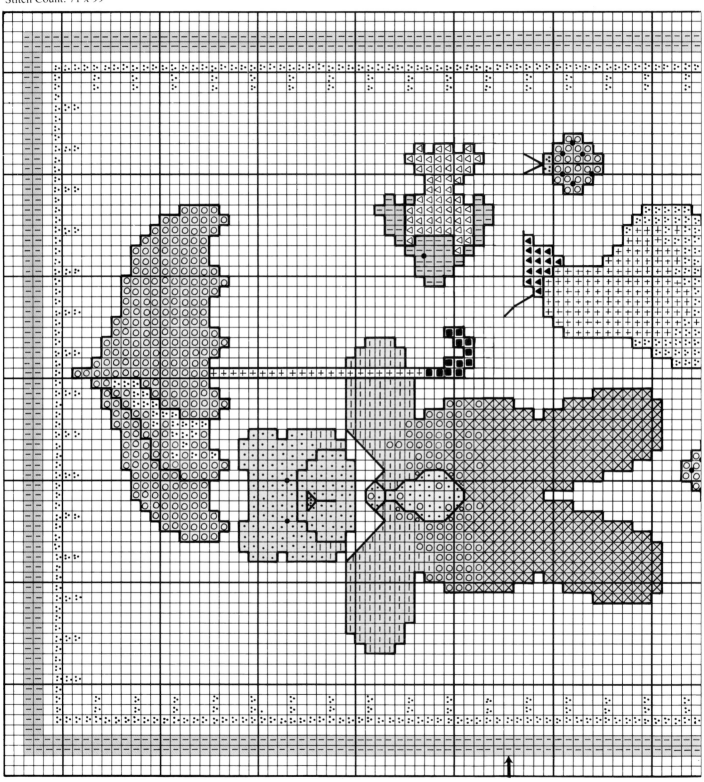

BABY'S SLEEPING

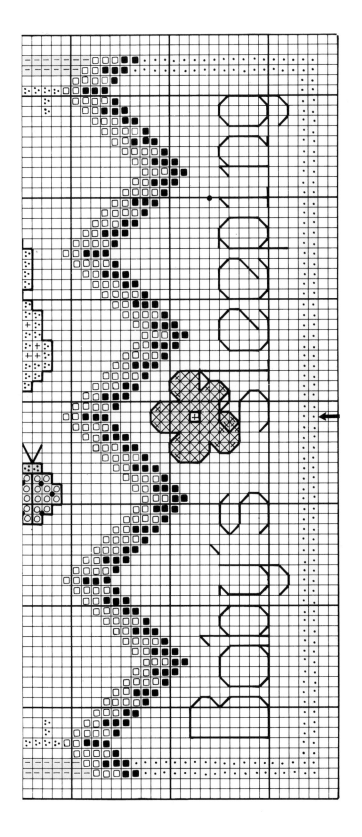

Stitched on Yellow Aida 14 over one thread, the finished design size is 5⅛" x 7⅛". The fabric was cut 10" x 12".

FABRIC	DESIGN SIZE
Aida 11	6½" x 9"
Aida 18	4" x 5½"
Hardanger 22	3¼" x 4½"

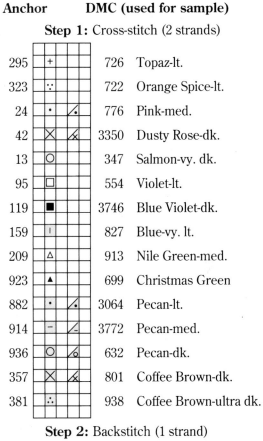

Anchor			DMC (used for sample)	
Step 1: Cross-stitch (2 strands)				
295	+		726	Topaz-lt.
323	∷		722	Orange Spice-lt.
24	·	⁄	776	Pink-med.
42	✕	⁄	3350	Dusty Rose-dk.
13	O		347	Salmon-vy. dk.
95	□		554	Violet-lt.
119	■		3746	Blue Violet-dk.
159	I		827	Blue-vy. lt.
209	△		913	Nile Green-med.
923	▲		699	Christmas Green
882	·	⁄	3064	Pecan-lt.
914	–	⁄	3772	Pecan-med.
936	O	⁄	632	Pecan-dk.
357	✕	⁄	801	Coffee Brown-dk.
381	∴		938	Coffee Brown-ultra dk.
Step 2: Backstitch (1 strand)				
381			938	Coffee Brown-ultra dk.
Step 3: French Knot (1 strand)				
381	●		938	Coffee Brown-ultra dk.

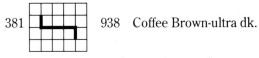

KICK UP YOUR HEELS

Stitched on White Murano 30 over two threads, the finished design size is 5¼" x 3⅜". The fabric was cut 14" x 11".

FABRIC	DESIGN SIZE
Aida 11	7⅛" x 4⅝"
Aida 14	5⅝" x 3⅝"
Aida 18	4⅜" x 2⅞"
Hardanger 22	3⅝" x 2⅜"

Supplies

Completed design on White Murano 30;
    matching thread
9⅝" x 6¾" piece of unstitched White Murano 30
⅛ yard of blue-and-white print fabric;
    matching thread
1 yard of narrow cording
Six assorted colored buttons
Stuffing

Directions

All seams are ¼".

1. Trim design piece to 9⅝" x 6¾" for pillow front. From print fabric, cut 1¼"-wide bias strips, piecing as needed to equal 1 yard. Make corded piping.

2. Using white thread, sew buttons to pillow front as desired; see photo.

3. With right sides facing and raw edges aligned, stitch piping around all edges of pillow front. With right sides facing, stitch pillow front to pillow back, sewing along stitching line of piping and leaving an opening on one seam. Trim corners and turn.

4. Stuff moderately with stuffing. Slipstitch opening closed.

Anchor		DMC (used for sample)	

Step 1: Cross-stitch (2 strands)

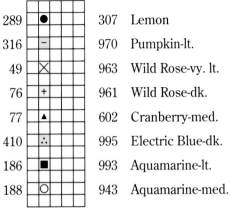

Anchor		DMC	
289	●	307	Lemon
316	–	970	Pumpkin-lt.
49	✕	963	Wild Rose-vy. lt.
76	+	961	Wild Rose-dk.
77	▲	602	Cranberry-med.
410	∴	995	Electric Blue-dk.
186	■	993	Aquamarine-lt.
188	○	943	Aquamarine-med.

Step 2: Backstitch (1 strand)

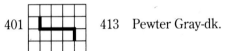

401		413	Pewter Gray-dk.

Step 3: French Knot (1 strand)

401	●	413	Pewter Gray-dk.

BEDROOMS

Stitch Count: 79 x 51

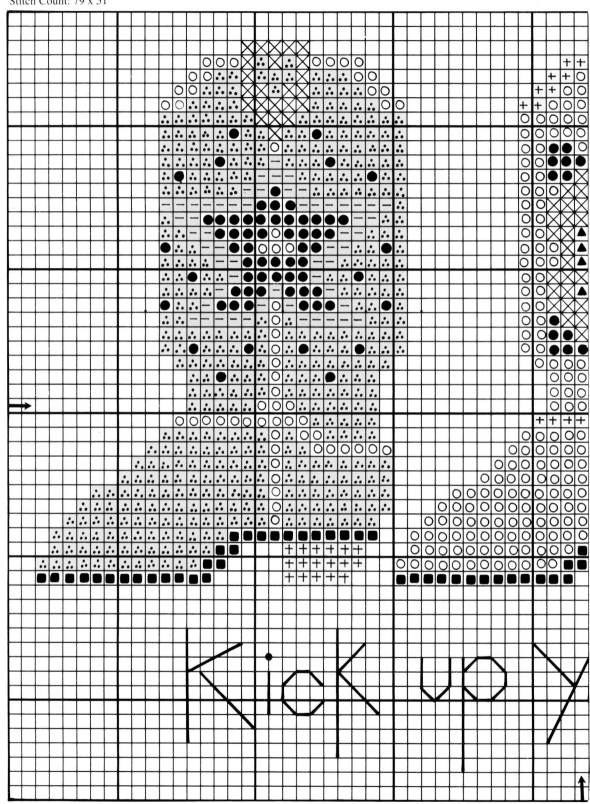

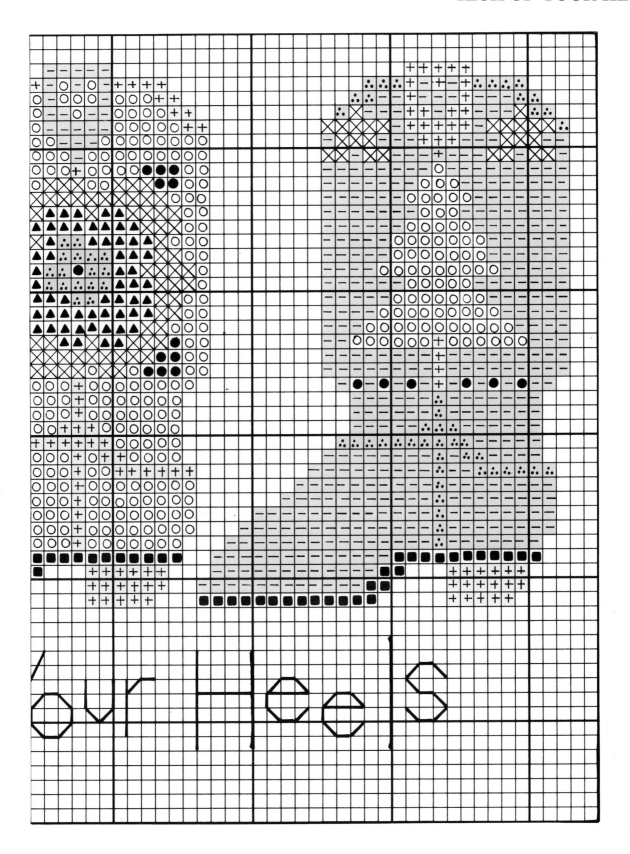

CHRISTMAS CANDLESCREEN

Stitched on White Belfast Linen 32 over two threads, the finished design size is 5⅛" x 6⅜". The fabric was cut 10" x 12". Insert design piece in candlescreen, following manufacturer's instructions.

FABRIC	DESIGN SIZE
Aida 11	7½" x 9¼"
Aida 14	5⅞" x 7¼"
Aida 18	4½" x 5⅝"
Hardanger 22	3¾" x 4⅝"

Anchor   DMC (used for sample)

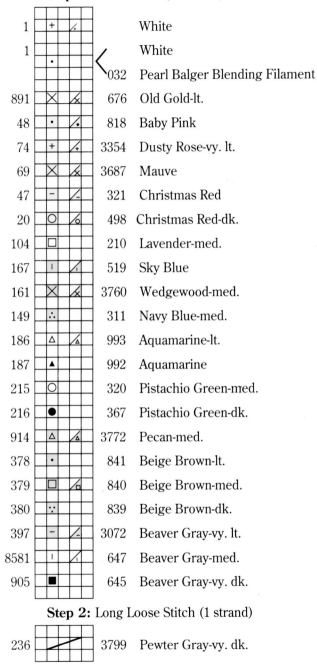

Step 1: Cross-stitch (2 strands)

Anchor	DMC	Name
1		White
1		White
	032	Pearl Balger Blending Filament
891	676	Old Gold-lt.
48	818	Baby Pink
74	3354	Dusty Rose-vy. lt.
69	3687	Mauve
47	321	Christmas Red
20	498	Christmas Red-dk.
104	210	Lavender-med.
167	519	Sky Blue
161	3760	Wedgewood-med.
149	311	Navy Blue-med.
186	993	Aquamarine-lt.
187	992	Aquamarine
215	320	Pistachio Green-med.
216	367	Pistachio Green-dk.
914	3772	Pecan-med.
378	841	Beige Brown-lt.
379	840	Beige Brown-med.
380	839	Beige Brown-dk.
397	3072	Beaver Gray-vy. lt.
8581	647	Beaver Gray-med.
905	645	Beaver Gray-vy. dk.

Step 2: Long Loose Stitch (1 strand)

236	3799	Pewter Gray-vy. dk.

Step 3: Backstitch (1 strand)

236	3799	Pewter Gray-vy. dk.

Stitch Count: 82 x 102

BEAR CLOCK

BEDROOMS

Stitched on White Aida 14 over one thread, the finished design size is 8¾" x 11¼". The fabric was cut 15" x 18". Insert design piece in clock, following manufacturer's instructions.

FABRIC	DESIGN SIZE
Aida 11	11⅛" x 14¼"
Aida 18	6⅞" x 8¾"
Hardanger 22	5⅝" x 7⅛"

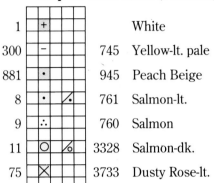

Anchor			DMC (used for sample)	

Step 1: Cross-stitch (2 strands)

Anchor			DMC	
1	+			White
300	−		745	Yellow-lt. pale
881	•		945	Peach Beige
8	•	╱	761	Salmon-lt.
9	∴		760	Salmon
11	O	╱	3328	Salmon-dk.
75	✕		3733	Dusty Rose-lt.

Stitch Count: 123 x 157

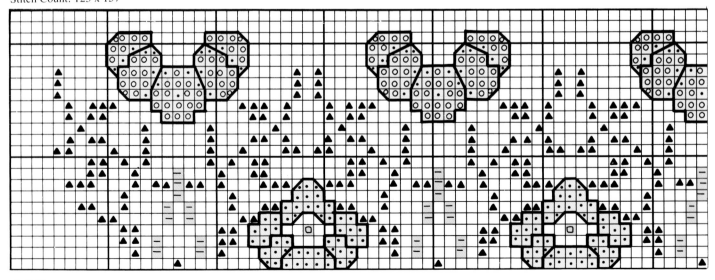

95	☒ ⊠	554	Violet-lt.
101	■	327	Antique Violet-vy. dk.
920	–	932	Antique Blue-lt.
978	☐	322	Navy Blue-vy. lt.
860	▲	3053	Green Gray
914	I ╱	3064	Pecan-lt.
905	●	3031	Mocha Brown-vy. dk.
397	○	3072	Beaver Gray-vy. lt.

Step 2: Backstitch (1 strand)

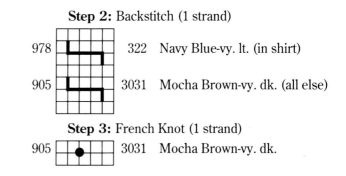

978		322	Navy Blue-vy. lt. (in shirt)
905		3031	Mocha Brown-vy. dk. (all else)

Step 3: French Knot (1 strand)

905	●	3031	Mocha Brown-vy. dk.

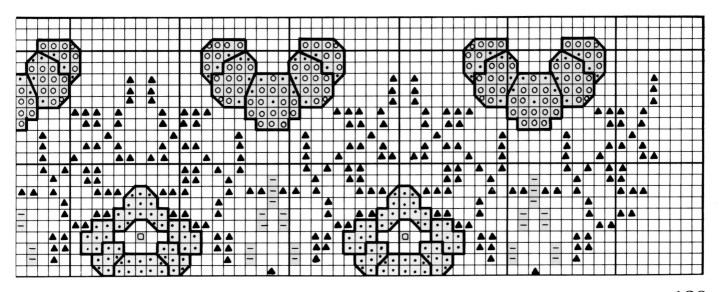

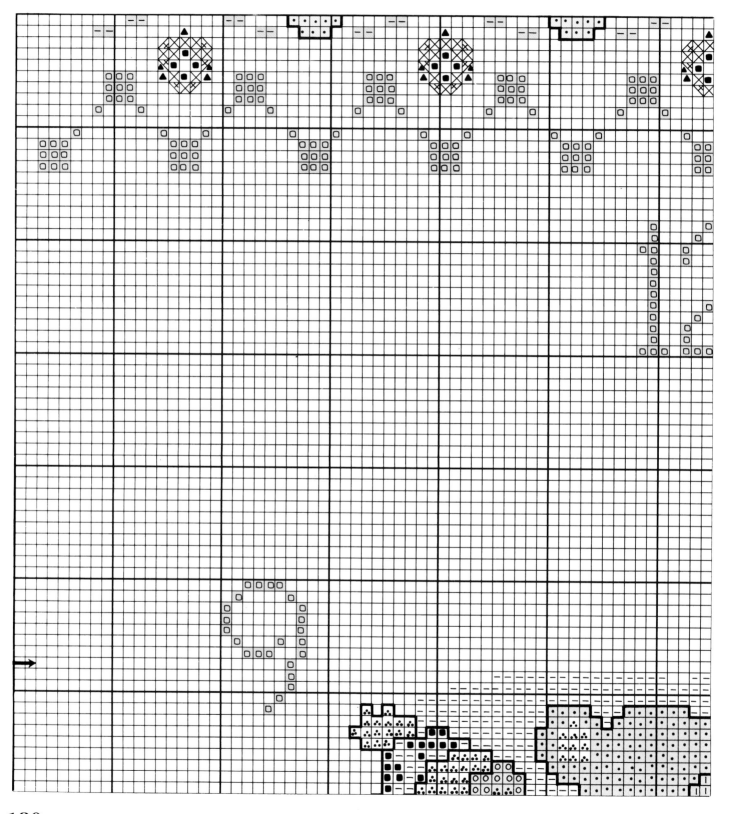

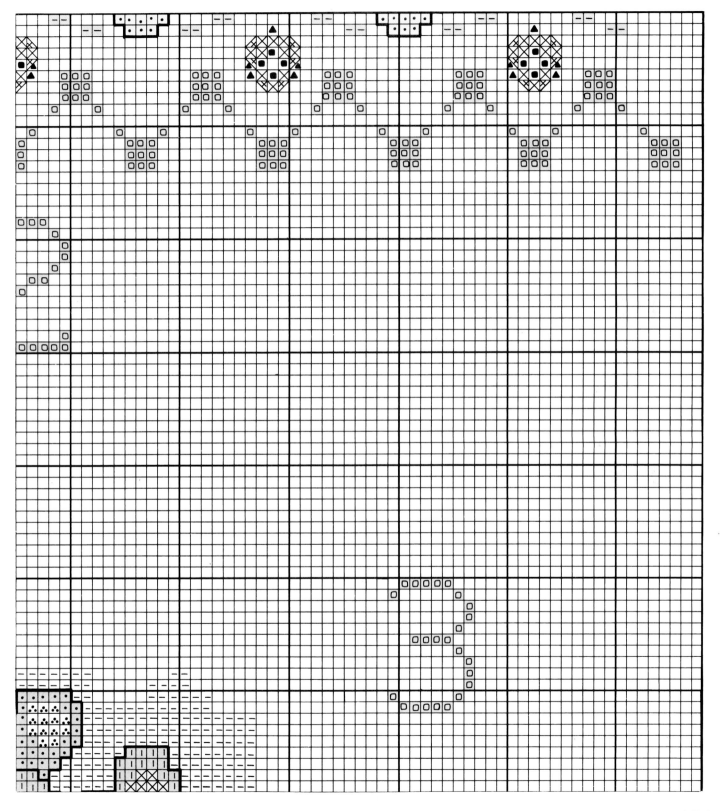

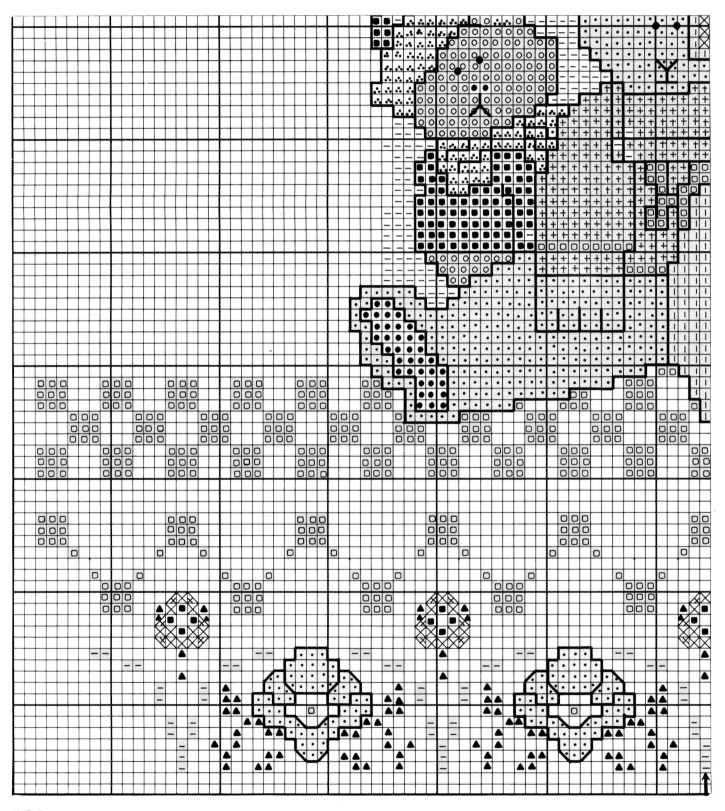

LES ANIMAUX

LE CHAT

Stitch Count: 80 x 80

LE LAPIN

Stitch Count: 80 x 80

Le Chat is stitched on Green Antique Linen 28 over two threads. Le Lapin is stitched on Blue Antique Linen 28 over 2 threads. Le Oie is stitched on Lavender Antique Linen 28 over two threads. Each finished design size is 5¾" x 5¾". The fabric was cut 12" x 12" for each.

FABRIC	DESIGN SIZE
Aida 11	7¼" x 7¼"
Aida 14	5¾" x 5¾"
Aida 18	4½" x 4½"
Hardanger 22	3⅝" x 3⅝"

LE CHAT

Anchor   **DMC (used for sample)**

Step 1: Cross-stitch (2 strands)

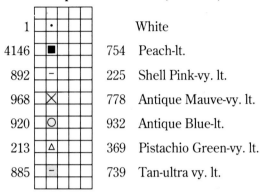

Anchor	DMC	(used for sample)
1		White
4146	754	Peach-lt.
892	225	Shell Pink-vy. lt.
968	778	Antique Mauve-vy. lt.
920	932	Antique Blue-lt.
213	369	Pistachio Green-vy. lt.
885	739	Tan-ultra vy. lt.

Step 2: Backstitch (1 strand)

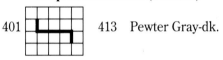

401	413	Pewter Gray-dk.

LE OIE

Anchor   **DMC (used for sample)**

Step 1: Cross-stitch (2 strands)

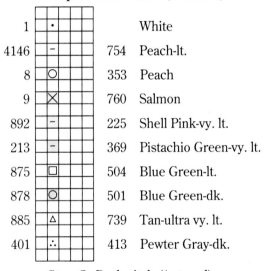

Anchor	DMC	(used for sample)
1		White
4146	754	Peach-lt.
8	353	Peach
9	760	Salmon
892	225	Shell Pink-vy. lt.
213	369	Pistachio Green-vy. lt.
875	504	Blue Green-lt.
878	501	Blue Green-dk.
885	739	Tan-ultra vy. lt.
401	413	Pewter Gray-dk.

Step 2: Backstitch (1 strand)

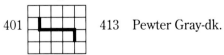

401	413	Pewter Gray-dk.

Step 3: French Knot (1 strand)

401	413	Pewter Gray-dk.

LE LAPIN

Anchor   **DMC (used for sample)**

Step 1: Cross-stitch (2 strands)

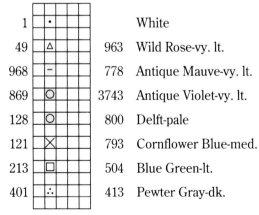

Anchor	DMC	(used for sample)
1		White
49	963	Wild Rose-vy. lt.
968	778	Antique Mauve-vy. lt.
869	3743	Antique Violet-vy. lt.
128	800	Delft-pale
121	793	Cornflower Blue-med.
213	504	Blue Green-lt.
401	413	Pewter Gray-dk.

Step 2: Backstitch (1 strand)

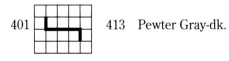

401	413	Pewter Gray-dk.

Step 3: French Knot (1 strand)

401	413	Pewter Gray-dk.

LE OIE

Stitch Count: 80 x 80

CROSS-STITCH

Fabrics: Counted cross-stitch is usually worked on even-weave fabric. These fabrics are manufactured specifically for counted thread embroidery and are woven with the same number of vertical as horizontal threads per inch. Because the number of threads in the fabric is equal in each direction, each stitch will be the same size. It is the number of threads per inch in even-weave fabrics that determines the size of a finished design.

Waste Canvas:
Waste canvas is a coarse, fabric-like substance used as a guide for cross-stitching on fabrics other than even-weaves. Cut the waste canvas 1" larger on all sides than the finished design size. Baste it to the fabric to be stitched. Complete the stitching. Then, dampen the stitched area with cold water. Pull the waste canvas threads out one at a time with tweezers. It is easier to pull all the threads running in one direction first, then pull out the opposite threads. Allow the stitching to dry. Place face down on a towel and iron.

Preparing Fabric:
Cut even-weave fabric at least 3" larger on all sides than the design size, or cut it the size specified in the instructions. If the item is to be finished into a pillow, for example, the fabric should be cut as directed. A 3" margin is the minimum amount of space that allows for comfortably working the edges of the design. To prevent fraying, whipstitch or machine-zigzag raw fabric edges.

Needles:
Needles should slip easily through the holes in the fabric but not pierce the fabric. Use a blunt tapestry needle, size 24 or 26. Never leave the needle in the design area of your work. It can leave rust or a permanent impression on the fabric.

Floss:
All numbers and color names are cross-referenced between Anchor and DMC brands of floss. Run the floss over a damp sponge to straighten. Separate all six strands and use the number of strands called for in the code.

Centering the Design:
Fold the fabric in half horizontally, then vertically. Place a pin in the fold point to mark the center. Locate the center of the design on the graph by following the vertical and horizontal arrows in the left and bottom margins. Begin stitching all designs at the center point of the graph and the fabric unless the instructions indicate otherwise.

Graphs:
Each symbol represents a different color. Make one stitch for each symbol, referring to the code to verify which stitch to use. Use the small arrows in the margins to find the center of the graph. When a graph is continued, the bottom two rows of the graph on the previous page are repeated, separated by a small space, indicating where to connect them. The stitch count is printed with each graph, listing first the width, then the length, of the design.

GENERAL INSTRUCTIONS

Codes: The code indicates the brand of thread used to stitch the model, as well as the cross-reference for using another brand. The steps in the code identify the stitch to be used and the number of floss strands for that stitch. The symbols match the graph, and give the color number and name for the thread. A symbol under a diagonal line indicates a half cross-stitch. Blended threads are represented on the code and graph with a single symbol, but both color names are listed.

Securing the Floss: Insert your needle up from the underside of the fabric at your starting point. Hold 1" of thread behind the fabric and stitch over it, securing with the first few stitches. To finish thread, run under four or more stitches on the back of the design. Never knot floss unless working on clothing. Another method of securing floss is the waste knot. Knot your floss and insert your needle from the right side of the fabric about 1" from design area. Work several stitches over the thread to secure. Cut off the knot later.

Stitching: For a smooth cross-stitch, use the "push-and-pull" method. Push the needle straight down and completely through fabric before pulling. Do not pull the thread tightly. Consistent tension throughout ensures even stitches. Make one stitch for every symbol on the chart. To stitch in rows, work from left to right and then back. Half-crosses are used to make a rounded shape. Make the longer stitch in the direction of the slanted line.

Carrying Floss: To carry floss, weave floss under the previously worked stitches on the back. Do not carry thread across any fabric that is not or will not be stitched. Loose threads, especially dark ones, will show through the fabric.

Twisted Floss: If floss is twisted, drop the needle and allow the floss to unwind itself. Floss will cover best when lying flat. Use thread no longer than 18" because it will tend to twist and knot.

Cleaning Completed Work: When stitching is complete, soak it in cold water with a mild soap for five to ten minutes. Rinse well and roll in a towel to remove excess water. Do not wring. Place work face down on a dry towel and iron on a warm setting until dry.

Cross-stitch: Make one cross for each symbol on the chart. Bring needle and thread up at A, down at B, up at C, and down again at D. For rows, stitch from left to right, then back. All stitches should lie in the same direction.

Half Cross-stitch:
The stitch actually fits three-fourths of the area. Make the longer stitch in the direction of the slanted line on the graph. Bring needle and thread up at A, down at B, up at C, and down at D.

Backstitch:
Complete all cross-stitching before working backstitches or other accent stitches. Working from left to right with one strand of floss (unless designated otherwise on code), bring needle and thread up at A, down at B, and up again at C. Go back down at A and continue in this manner.

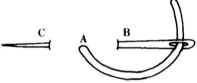

French Knot:
Bring needle up at A, using one strand of embroidery floss. Wrap floss around needle two times (unless indicated otherwise in instructions). Insert needle beside A, pulling floss until it fits snugly around needle. Pull needle through to back.

SEWING HINTS

Patterns:
Use tracing paper to trace patterns. Be sure to transfer all information. All patterns include seam allowances. The seam allowance is ¼" unless otherwise specified.

Marking on Fabric:
Always use a dressmaker's pen or chalk to mark on fabric. It will wash out when you clean your finished piece.

Slipstitch:
Insert needle at A, taking a small stitch, and slide it through the folded edge of the fabric about ⅛" to ¼", bringing it out at B.

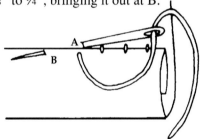

Enlarging a Pattern:
On a sheet of paper large enough to hold the finished pattern, mark grid lines 1" apart to fill the paper. Begin marking dots on 1" grid lines where the reduced pattern intersects the corresponding grid line. Connect the dots. Fabric stores sell pattern-making products which can save a great deal of time.

Bias Strips:
Bias strips are used for ruffles, binding or corded piping. To cut bias, fold the fabric at a 45-degree angle to the grain of the fabric and crease. Cut on the crease. Cut additional strips the width indicated in the instructions and parallel to the first cutting line. The ends of the bias strips should be on the grain of the fabric. Place the right sides of the ends together and stitch with a ¼" seam. Continue to piece the strips until they are the length that is indicated in the instructions.

Corded Piping:
Center cording on the wrong side of the bias strip and fold the fabric over it, aligning raw edges. Using a zipper foot, stitch through both layers of fabric close to the cording. Trim the seam allowance to ¼".

Mitering a Corner:
Sew border strips up to but not through, the seam allowance; backstitch. Repeat on all four edges, making stitching lines meet exactly at the corners. Fold two adjacent border pieces together. Mark, then stitch at a 45-degree angle. Trim seam allowance to ¼".

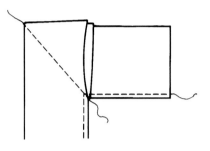

MM-Millimetres   CM-Centimetres

INCHES TO MILLIMETRES AND CENTIMETRES

INCHES	MM	CM	INCHES	CM	INCHES	CM
⅛	3	0.3	9	22.9	30	76.2
¼	6	0.6	10	25.4	31	78.7
⅜	10	1.0	11	27.9	32	81.3
½	13	1.3	12	30.5	33	83.8
⅝	16	1.6	13	33.0	34	86.4
¾	19	1.9	14	35.6	35	88.9
⅞	22	2.2	15	38.1	36	91.4
1	25	2.5	16	40.6	37	94.0
1¼	32	3.2	17	43.2	38	96.5
1½	38	3.8	18	45.7	39	99.1
1¾	44	4.4	19	48.3	40	101.6
2	51	5.1	20	50.8	41	104.1
2½	64	6.4	21	53.3	42	106.7
3	76	7.6	22	55.9	43	109.2
3½	89	8.9	23	58.4	44	111.8
4	102	10.2	24	61.0	45	114.3
4½	114	11.4	25	63.5	46	116.8
5	127	12.7	26	66.0	47	119.4
6	152	15.2	27	68.6	48	121.9
7	178	17.8	28	71.1	49	124.5
8	203	20.3	29	73.7	50	127.0

YARDS TO METRES

YARDS	METRES	YARDS	METRES	YARDS	METRES	YARDS	METRES	YARDS	METRES
⅛	0.11	2⅛	1.94	4⅛	3.77	6⅛	5.60	8⅛	7.43
¼	0.23	2¼	2.06	4¼	3.89	6¼	5.72	8¼	7.54
⅜	0.34	2⅜	2.17	4⅜	4.00	6⅜	5.83	8⅜	7.66
½	0.46	2½	2.29	4½	4.11	6½	5.94	8½	7.77
⅝	0.57	2⅝	2.40	4⅝	4.23	6⅝	6.06	8⅝	7.89
¾	0.69	2¾	2.51	4¾	4.34	6¾	6.17	8¾	8.00
⅞	0.80	2⅞	2.63	4⅞	4.46	6⅞	6.29	8⅞	8.12
1	0.91	3	2.74	5	4.57	7	6.40	9	8.23
1⅛	1.03	3⅛	2.86	5⅛	4.69	7⅛	6.52	9⅛	8.34
1¼	1.14	3¼	2.97	5¼	4.80	7¼	6.63	9¼	8.46
1⅜	1.26	3⅜	3.09	5⅜	4.91	7⅜	6.74	9⅜	8.57
1½	1.37	3½	3.20	5½	5.03	7½	6.86	9½	8.69
1⅝	1.49	3⅝	3.31	5⅝	5.14	7⅝	6.97	9⅝	8.80
1¾	1.60	3¾	3.43	5¾	5.26	7¾	7.09	9¾	8.92
1⅞	1.71	3⅞	3.54	5⅞	5.37	7⅞	7.20	9⅞	9.03
2	1.83	4	3.66	6	5.49	8	7.32	10	9.14

144